The Librarian's Guide to
Academic Research in the Cloud

CHANDOS
INFORMATION PROFESSIONAL SERIES

Series Editor: Ruth Rikowski
(email: Rikowskigr@aol.com)

Chandos' new series of books is aimed at the busy information professional. They have been specially commissioned to provide the reader with an authoritative view of current thinking. They are designed to provide easy-to-read and (most importantly) practical coverage of topics that are of interest to librarians and other information professionals. If you would like a full listing of current and forthcoming titles, please visit our website, www.chandospublishing.com, email wp@woodheadpublishing.com or telephone +44 (0) 1223 499140.

New authors: we are always pleased to receive ideas for new titles; if you would like to write a book for Chandos, please contact Dr Glyn Jones on gjones@chandospublishing.com or telephone +44 (0) 1993 848726.

Bulk orders: some organisations buy a number of copies of our books. If you are interested in doing this, we would be pleased to discuss a discount. Please email wp@woodheadpublishing.com or telephone +44 (0) 1223 499140.

The Librarian's Guide to Academic Research in the Cloud

STEVEN OVADIA

Oxford Cambridge New Delhi

Chandos Publishing
Hexagon House
Avenue 4
Station Lane
Witney
Oxford OX28 4BN
UK
Tel: +44 (0) 1993 848726
Email: info@chandospublishing.com
www.chandospublishing.com
www.chandospublishingonline.com

Chandos Publishing is an imprint of Woodhead Publishing Limited

Woodhead Publishing Limited
80 High Street
Sawston
Cambridge CB22 3HJ
UK
Tel: +44 (0) 1223 499140
Fax: +44 (0) 1223 832819
www.woodheadpublishing.com

First published in 2013

ISBN: 978-1-84334-715-6 (print)
ISBN: 978-1-78063-381-7 (online)

Chandos Information Professional Series ISSN: 2052-210X (print) and ISSN: 2052-2118 (online)
Library of Congress Control Number: 2013942533

British Library Cataloguing-in-Publication Data.
A catalogue record for this book is available from the British Library.

Typeset by Domex e-Data Pvt. Ltd., India

Dedicated to Jenny,
my sunshine in the clouds

Contents

List of figures   xiii

Glossary   xv

Acknowledgements   xxi

About the author   xxiii

1   **Introduction to the cloud**   **1**

2   **Capturing information**   **11**

    Delicious   13

    Pinboard   15

    Diigo   17

    Browser bookmark syncing   19

    Evernote   21

    Springpad   24

    Postponed reading services   26

    OneNote   29

    Conclusion   31

3   **Capturing and managing scholarly information**   **33**

    How do researchers keep track of scholarly research?   35

    RefWorks   35

    Mendeley   39

    Zotero   43

    CiteULike   45

    EndNote   47

	Papers	49
	Subscription databases	52
	BibTeX	55
	Conclusion	56
4	**Storing files in the cloud**	**59**
	Dropbox	60
	SpiderOak	66
	Google Drive	68
	Box	70
	Ubuntu One	73
	SugarSync	75
	SkyDrive	76
	ownCloud	78
	iCloud	79
	Conclusion	80
5	**Writing in the cloud**	**83**
	Google Drive	85
	Microsoft Word Web App	89
	Zoho Writer	91
	PBworks	92
	Simplenote	95
	Yahoo! Notepad	97
	Sharing files	98
	Conclusion	100
6	**Staying organized**	**103**
	Web-based calendars	104
	Remember the Milk	109
	Basecamp	111
	Google Tasks	114

	Trello	116
	Asana	117
	Mac productivity	119
	Conclusion	122
7	**Communicating**	**127**
	Managing email	128
	Instant messaging	132
	Video chat	137
	IRC	139
	Conclusion	143
8	**Sharing**	**147**
	Blogs	148
	Microblogs	155
	Nameplates	161
	Conclusion	163
9	**The future of the cloud**	**167**
	Consolidation of features	168
	Consolidation of customers	170
	Consolidation of services	172
	Return to local services	173
	Thin clients	175
	The rise of Linux	176
	Devices	177
	Conclusion	179
References		**183**
Index		**187**

List of figures

2.1	Delicious	13
2.2	Pinboard	16
2.3	Diigo	18
2.4	Evernote	22
2.5	Springpad	24
2.6	Pocket	27
2.7	OneNote	29
3.1	RefWorks	36
3.2	Mendeley	39
3.3	Zotero	43
3.4	CiteULike	46
3.5	EndNote	48
3.6	Papers	49
3.7	EBSCO	53
3.8	BibTeX	55
4.1	Dropbox	61
4.2	SpiderOak	66
4.3	Google Drive	69
4.4	Box	71
4.5	Ubuntu One	73
4.6	SugarSync	75

4.7	SkyDrive	77
4.8	ownCloud	78
5.1	Google Drive	86
5.2	Microsoft Word Web App	90
5.3	Zoho Writer	91
5.4	PBworks	92
5.5	Simplenote	95
5.6	Yahoo! Notepad	97
6.1	Outlook calendar	105
6.2	Remember the Milk	110
6.3	Basecamp	112
6.4	Google Tasks	115
6.5	Trello	116
6.6	Asana	118
6.7	OmniFocus	120
6.8	Things	121
7.1	AIM	133
7.2	Yahoo! Messenger	134
7.3	Pidgin	135
7.4	Skype	138
7.5	XChat	140
8.1	WordPress	150
8.2	Blogger	151
8.3	Tumblr	156
8.4	Twitter	158
8.5	about.me	162

Glossary

AIM
AOL Instant Messenger: one of the earliest real-time chat tools, which is still used today. AIM exists as a client and as a cloud-based chat tool

Apps
Short for applications, the term usually applies to software for mobile devices and tablets. It is also sometimes used to refer to website or browser enhancements. For example, the Chrome browser store calls its browser extensions apps.

BibTeX
The citation file format associated with the LaTeX markup language. BibTeX allows LaTeX users to integrate references into the larger work. Many subscription databases, as well as free tools, such as Google Scholar, allow users to export citations in BibTeX. Most citation managers allow users to import BibTeX citations.

Bookmarklet
A web browser bookmark that can be used to import web page metadata into a cloud-based tool. Where most bookmarks bring users to a page, bookmarklets bring page data to a tool.

CalDAV   A standard for web-based calendars, the format allows users to sync calendars across devices, both client- and web-based.

Client   Downloaded software used to interface with a cloud-based service. Many cloud services allow users to interact either via a client or via a web browser.

.doc   The Microsoft file format for word-processed documents.

.docx   The current Microsoft file format for word-processed documents (as of Word 2007).

DOI   Digital object identifier: a unique alphanumeric string, which can be used to locate academic content online, using the CrossRef service (*www.crossref.org*). Users with an article DOI can enter it into CrossRef, where they'll be taken to the article, assuming they're entitled to access.

.ics   The iCalendar file format. Many web- and client-based calendars allow users to import and export data in this format.

IM   Instant messaging: the process of real-time text chat, usually between two people.

iOS   Apple's mobile operating system, used on iPhones and iPads.

IRB   A college- or university-wide committee that reviews and approves all research involving humans.

IRC   Internet Relay Chat: a protocol that allows users to chat either as a group or one-on-one. Users communicate by connecting to specific IRC servers. Once connected to a server, users communicate in areas called rooms.

ISBN International Standard Book Number: a unique number used to identify books.

JSON JavaScript Object Notation: a commonly used format for web-based data. Certain cloud-based tools allow users to export their data in this format, which is human-readable.

LaTeX A markup language used to format documents, usually equation-driven scholarship, but not exclusive to it.

Metadata A broad term for subject headings used to describe electronic data. They frequently include fields such as title, author, and publication date.

.mht A file format used to represent entire captured web pages in one file, including images. Users saving a web page in Internet Explorer will wind up with an .mht file, which becomes a locally-hosted version of the saved page.

.odt The OpenDocument text document format: commonly used in open source word processors such as LibreOffice and Apache OpenOffice (formerly OpenOffice.org).

Operating system The software used to control computer hardware. Examples include Windows 7,

	Mac OS X, and Linux. Mobile operating systems include Android and iOS.
PDF	Portable document format: PDFs are files that cannot be edited in the same way as traditional text-based, word-processed documents. Instead, they are more designed to preserve the formatting of a document, so the document renders consistently across software and hardware.
PMID	PubMed Identifier: the unique number assigned to PubMed database documents.
RIS	A citation file format. Certain subscription collections allow users to export citations in this format and many citation management tools are able to import these files.
RSS	Rich Site Summary: allows users to import content across sites into a centralized reader. Many subscription databases allow users to create RSS feeds of searches, with search results showing up in the centralized reader.
.rtf	Rich Text Format: a common and portable word-processed document format that tends to work well across different word processors.
.sxw	The precursor to the OpenDocument format, these kinds of word-processed files are still seen as an option in many open source word processors, such as LibreOffice and Apache OpenOffice.

.txt The file extension for a text file: these very portable files support very little formatting, but can be opened with a multitude of tools across devices.

.wpd The file extension used to indicate WordPerfect documents.

XML Extensible Markup Language: a language used to describe web content. While most users do not work with XML directly, XML drives a lot of web-based tools, making it easy for information to be transmitted and shared.

Acknowledgements

The exploration of some of the ideas discussed in this book began as part of my work as "Internet Connections" columnist for the journal *Behavioral and Social Sciences Librarian*. I am very grateful to that journal, and to its editor, Professor Lisa Romero, for the opportunity it gave me to think about the role of cloud-based tools in academic work, and I'm grateful for this platform to expand the ideas. I am also indebted to my colleagues at LaGuardia Community College Library Media Resources Center for their kindness and support. I am especially indebted to my chair, Professor Jane Devine, who cleared a path that allowed me to finish this project.

This book would not have been possible without the new faculty reassignment leave negotiated by the Professional Staff Congress, the CUNY faculty union.

About the author

Steven Ovadia is Associate Professor/Web Services Librarian at LaGuardia Community College, City University of New York (CUNY). He frequently writes about how users interact with information in an online context. He is the Internet Connection columnist for *Behavioral & Social Sciences Librarian* and his work has been published in the *Journal of Academic Librarianship*, *Library Philosophy and Practice*, and *Journal of Web Librarianship*. Steven has an MLIS from Palmer School of Library and Information Science, and an MA in Applied Social Research from Queens College, CUNY.

Steven Ovadia can be contacted at: *sovadia@lagcc.cuny.edu*

Introduction to the cloud

Abstract: The cloud concept refers to software and data that is not hosted on a local computer or device, but instead that is available online. While a conventional word processor launches from software on a user's computer, a cloud-based one launches through a web browser. Cloud-based tools allow users to easily move between computers and devices, as files and services are not limited to a single local device, but instead are available anywhere there is, or was, an Internet connection. For academic users, this access promises to make work easier, allowing users to do serious research work from just about anywhere, without having to worry about where files or content are located. It also promises to simplify collaboration. However, users still need to be concerned about issues related to the cloud, such as the privacy of files and the portability of the data users hold in the cloud.

Key words: academic research, cloud, files, locally hosted, operating system, portability, privacy.

Imagine someone writing a book chapter. They want feedback on the chapter from some colleagues. They could easily print a hard copy and give it to the colleagues. But if some of the colleagues are far away, the user would need to either mail paper copies to the distant colleagues or distribute the file by email. Either way, none of the reviewers could see the comments of the others. It would be incumbent upon the writer to synthesize and input all of the changes. And if they decided to go over changes on the fly, perhaps while visiting yet another colleague, they would need either to take the electronic files with them or to download them from email. This is a workable labor flow, but hardly an ideal one.

Contrast that with the writer sharing their work via a link emailed to their colleagues, both distant and far, with the colleagues able to make their changes and suggestions directly on the original work, and each person's changes displaying in a different color. Reviewers could see the work of other reviewers and the writer would have everything in one document. If they wanted to show the working document to another colleague, all they would need to do is log into a site and show the colleague the document in a web browser, with no downloading or flash drives required. This is the power of the cloud.

The cloud concept refers to programs and services that are hosted online, rather than on a local machine. Instead of something like a word processor being run from software hosted on a laptop or desktop, a cloud-based word processor runs from a program hosted on servers that are accessible online. For users of a certain vintage, the concept is familiar: in the days of mainframes, terminals often ran programs hosted on the central mainframe, rather than software hosted on the local terminal on which the user was working.

What can be confusing about the cloud concept is that most users simply do not realize when they are using a cloud-based service. Many users click an icon or open a web page, do their work, and don't think about where the program or files are actually hosted. Many cloud services have become so good that users do not necessarily need to even consider that the program they are using is being accessed from servers that might be physically located halfway around the world.

The cloud has become an important tool for all knowledge workers, including academics, but especially librarians. The cloud concept provides a number of advantages for users. In general, cloud-based services make it easier for users to collaborate in ways that are not possible with locally hosted software (although, as will be discussed in this book, there is more and more locally hosted software that has cloud functionality). Cloud-based services are also consistently available across computers and devices. For users invested in cloud services, this means never having that feeling of realizing a crucial file has been left on another computer. On a more practical level, it also often allows users to dispense with the thumb drive full of files that are moved from computer to computer, which is dependable – usually right up until the moment the drive is misplaced. Cloud-based services are also quite helpful for times when local hard drives die, providing users with a backup of their work that is immune from stolen laptops and spilled coffee.

While not everyone has rushed to embrace the cloud, a 2010 Pew Internet report found 71 per cent of respondents, all technology experts of some kind from diverse fields, agreed with the idea that by 2020 most users will work via cloud-hosted services and not locally hosted ones (Anderson and Rainie, 2010). Conversely, 27 per cent of respondents said they didn't see most people moving their work to the cloud by 2020.

The precise future of the cloud remains to be seen, but there is no denying that more users, even academic ones, are gravitating toward cloud-based services because of their prevalence and convenience. This particular convergence places librarians in an interesting position. Many academic librarians are actively involved in publishing, so they are using these tools to manage and facilitate their own work. At the same time, many academic librarians also serve as de facto technology advisers on their campus, helping faculty outside the library to understand the technology that helps to drive the research process. This allows librarians to not only use these cloud-based tools for their own work, but also to shape how their colleagues use them. This is especially important given that many of the tools discussed within this book are designed to help users work with subscription research tools, such as e-book and scholarly article collections. Librarians working with these cloud-based tools will also find themselves with the opportunity to show colleagues outside the library the power and utility of subscription research tools, helping many to go beyond simple Google searches.

Cloud migration is also driven by the increase in Internet-enabled devices. It is probably a given that most academics have access to a computer and Internet connection, if not at home then certainly from on campus. But as users gather and work across more devices, it can become challenging for users to keep their work in sync. The data seems to indicate that more users are going online using mobile devices. Another Pew study reported 17 per cent of all cell phone owners go online mostly using their phones, while about a third mostly go online with another device, even if they do access the Internet on their phone (Smith, 2012). The Pew data also indicates 55 per cent of adult cell phone owners go online using their mobile devices, with Internet usage via cell phone seeming to be trending upward. While it is unlikely many academics are doing serious work on their cell phones, it seems more adults are using them to do something online. With more cell phone users online, it seems logical that an increasing amount of academic research work will eventually be conducted using a mobile device, if only to read a saved article or quickly double-check a citation. Factor in Internet-enabled tablets, which Pew puts at 19 per cent ownership in the United States, and the potential for cloud-based services to make it possible for users to work effectively across different devices can readily be seen (Rainie, 2012).

It is with these variables converging that this book has been written. Cloud-based services are necessary for the increasing number of users who are working across devices. It's not that the concept of a local machine no longer makes sense. Instead, it seems that the concept of a *single* local machine is becoming an outdated one for many users.

This book is intended to provide a framework for understanding cloud-based services, using specific, active (as of this writing) tools as a point of departure. As with anything Internet-based, this is very much a moving target, as services change very quickly. Features that exist today might not exist tomorrow. Services that exist today, might not exist tomorrow. And new services are being created all the time. The point of this book is not to perfectly capture a moment in time, nor is it to exhaustively capture and document every service. Instead, this book is an attempt to guide readers in how to think about the cloud and to describe features and workflow that will be helpful for academic users. In all likelihood the features of certain services will change over time. But the utility of those features will not change. So even if certain services described within this book no longer have certain features, the user should still be able to find a service with the features they need. This work mentions specific tools, but the user would be advised to focus more on the features within the tools. The reality of these services is that they are ephemeral. There is no way to accurately predict which services will survive over time. This makes writing (and reading) about them challenging.

The ephemeral nature of these services is also a challenge for the end-user. Local software, for the most part, is permanent. Software vendors go out of business constantly, but anything installed on a local computer will always be on the local computer, for the life of the local computer. The vendor may cease to update the software, or **operating system** changes may render software unusable, but the software itself will always reside on the local machine. When a cloud service goes out of business, the service disappears. There is no way for a user to continue to use a cloud service that no longer exists. There is no way to keep a local copy of the service.

The loss of a service is frustrating, but users should probably be more concerned about what happens to their data when a service goes out of business. If they have no locally saved copy of their work, they could potentially lose everything they have saved in the cloud. If the cloud is a user's only source for their work, they are only marginally better off than they would be with their data saved to only a local drive. In terms of protecting information, redundancy is very important. Important information must be saved in multiple places.

Even if a service does not disappear, users often wish to switch to another service. That brings up the issue of data portability. Services make it very easy to upload and create content, but not all make it easy to extract content. So even if a service does not go out of business, that does not guarantee users will have persistent access to their own work. For instance, a cloud-based service might move from a free model to a paid model. This could force users to pay for access to their work, with the users' content essentially held hostage by a service. Users should always have an exit strategy for their content. Before users invest too much time in a service, they should be sure there is a way to easily and usefully export their data out of the service. Otherwise, they might be forced to stay with a service they would not ordinarily continue using, just to preserve access to their content. This is not usually an issue on locally hosted applications, because the user controls the machine on which the content is saved, but it is very much an issue with the cloud, especially when users do not have direct access to the server on which the service is hosted.

Another challenge of cloud-based services is privacy and security. Users probably want some level of security to protect their work from being viewed by others. But for cloud-based services, there are four potential viewers of information. The first two could be considered desirable viewers: the account holder themselves, who will need access to their work, and any collaborators, as selected by the account holder. The other two parties could be considered less desirable: the host of the service and the public at large (this manuscript will not address the perils of government surveillance, an important topic that is beyond the scope of this book). At the very least, users should make sure their content is protected against prying eyes. Is content only accessible with a password? If not, it's a good guess that anyone with a web address for a user's content will be able to access it. Depending upon the service and the content, this could have institutional review board (**IRB**) ramifications, because privacy is an important part of IRB compliance.

But even if content is not publicly accessible, the host still might have varying degrees of access to a user's data, whatever the data is. This has been an issue for a number of services, including Google. Some users do not care what data or information a vendor can view, while others want some assurances that their work is private. Users concerned about privacy, not only from outside a service, but also from the service itself, would do well to read the terms and conditions before using the service. Users might also keep in mind that unless they are personally securing data or servers themselves, they really cannot know just how safe or private their work is. Users might assume a certain level of security on their local machine that is not possible with cloud-hosted services, although local machines are vulnerable in their own ways.

This book will discuss the strengths and weaknesses of the various services from a privacy and data portability perspective, but, as mentioned earlier, services change very quickly. Users should instead use the discussions within this book as a point of departure for deciding whether a potential service is secure, private, and provides an easy way for data to be exported, should they decide they no longer wish to continue with the service. Also, users should always have a fallback option should a service suddenly be unavailable. For most users, this will be locally saved copies of the work that is in the cloud, but it could also be a secondary cloud service.

A final consideration when working with cloud services is that by nature they hinge, in some manner, on an Internet connection. Some cloud services have some functionality without an active Internet connection, but many do not. Users should consider Internet access when working with cloud-based services. If they will be working in an area without consistent Internet access, they might reconsider the utility of a cloud-based service. Users working on mobile devices should also consider their data plans. A limited data plan and a data-intensive cloud service could be a recipe for a very expensive bill.

Still, despite these potential challenges, the cloud is a fantastically convenient tool that is well worth the time investment, in terms of selecting tools that accomplish users' goals with the privacy and data portability they require.

The cloud services discussed within this book are, for the most part, operating system agnostic. This is yet another advantage of the cloud. Locally hosted software depends upon the operating system of the local machine: software built for OS X will not run on Windows. But with cloud-based tools, the operating system is often less of an issue, because most run through the browser, which very rarely depends upon the operating system on which the browser is installed. These browser-based tools prevent the drama and frustration caused by users worrying whether they have the right version of an operating system, or even the right operating system. Users don't have to declare that they are Mac or PC, or even Linux for that matter, but instead, in most cases, merely have to visit a website. Often, these browser-based versions of a tool will also be available from mobile browsers, giving users access across devices. This flexibility is useful, in that users have a wide variety of tools to choose from. But it also is very helpful in terms of collaboration. Cloud-based services not only facilitate collaboration by allowing users to access software on a central server to which all collaborators have access, but the browser-centric nature of so many of the tools means the local operating system is no longer an issue. If one user wishes to work on a cloud-based word processor using their OS X machine and another wishes to use their Linux machine, there is no issue. Both users can access the service via their browsers. They do not need to find a piece of software that can work between the two different operating systems. This allows users to focus on work rather than logistics, although, as will be demonstrated, there are still plenty of decisions to be made when selecting a cloud-based service. But the true advantage of the cloud is that it allows users to collaborate with themselves. The same features that facilitate collaboration between individuals are also helpful for users working alone between devices.

This book will identify services that are not cross-platform, although, as mentioned previously, that situation can change very quickly. This book also strives to identify mobile applications (**apps**), when tools have one available. Android and **iOS** are the most popular mobile platforms and apps enter and exit their respective markets fairly quickly. This book will not explore mobile tools in too much detail, but will alert readers to when relevant apps exist. But the assumption is that most academic users will not be doing serious work on a mobile device for at least the next few years, if not longer.

The cloud is a challenging environment in which to work, as will be described in the chapters that follow, but it also provides features that allow users to collaborate in ways that are not possible using locally hosted software. The cloud also provides the potential for users to protect their work by creating redundancy. As with any new concept, the cloud presents risks and rewards, not all of which are fully understood. However, the tools are still worth exploring, as long as users proceed thoughtfully and carefully. Users do not necessarily need to move all of their research tools into the cloud in one afternoon. Instead, they might think about the parts of their workflow that might benefit from the cloud and then explore some tools.

2

Capturing information

Abstract: Not all academic research relies on the capture of formal, scholarly material from books and electronic collections. Many researchers also need to capture non-scholarly content. This type of content can be more challenging to work with, in that the metadata is often less complete than is seen in formal works. Also, the high volume of non-scholarly material can be challenging to address. This chapter will discuss ways to capture and organize non-scholarly web-based material, covering simple, cloud-based bookmarking services such as Pinboard and Delicious, more robust capture tools such as Diigo, Evernote, Springpad, and OneNote, and postponed reading services, which allow users to quickly and easily mark something to be read later, but be accessible across a variety of devices. The chapter will also discuss ways to sync local browser-based bookmarks.

Key words: bookmark, Delicious, Diigo, EverNote, OneNote, Pinboard, postponed reading, Springpad, Xmarks.

The reality of contemporary research for many faculty is that it takes place within a web browser. The research process begins with gathering all data related to the project, such as submission guidelines, information on citation formats, and perhaps some web guides on where to look for research.

These kinds of materials are very much related to the development of an academic work, but are not themselves scholarly. For a myriad of reasons, non-scholarly sources like these need to be captured to facilitate retrieval at a later date.

This is not a new problem. The birth of the web browser was followed almost immediately by the birth of the bookmark, with bookmarks giving users a way to save URLs they might want to visit at a later date. The challenge of bookmarks is that they live on a local computer and within a particular browser. If a user bookmarks a page in Internet Explorer, they will not have access to that bookmark within Safari, unless they also bookmark the same page in Safari. If a page is bookmarked at home, the bookmark will not show up on a work computer.

Bookmarking also does not capture much **metadata** from a page. Most browser bookmarks simply capture a web address and the page title, without providing a way for the information to be annotated. This too can be limiting for users, especially ones who want to provide context or an explanation for whatever it was they just bookmarked.

This chapter will discuss cloud-based tools designed to facilitate the capture of non-scholarly web-based content (the capture of scholarly content is discussed in Chapter 3). The advantage of all of the cloud-based capture tools discussed in this chapter is that they allow users to have access to their bookmarks and annotations from just about any Internet-enabled device. This can be quite helpful when considering the ramifications of an important link or note being trapped in the browser of a machine a user cannot access, such as an office machine when someone is away on vacation or a home machine when someone is at work. Constant access to bookmarks does not seem important until it is needed. Then, it suddenly becomes a very important feature. For instance, author manuscript preparation instructions are often hidden deeply within publisher websites. If a user is trying to finish a manuscript, they might not want to spend time going through old emails and searching through a site. They probably want quicker access to the content in order to find what they need, rather than searching for what they need.

Delicious

Delicious (*www.delicious.com*) was one of the first cloud-hosted bookmarking services. Its concept is simple. Users use the Delicious web interface to bookmark sites, assigning tags and a brief description (Figure 2.1). The concept behind Delicious has not changed, but the company itself has seen some dramatic ups and downs that are worth mentioning only because they speak to the potential long-term viability of the company.

Founded in 2003, the company was sold to Yahoo! in 2005, but was never truly integrated into Yahoo!'s portfolio

Figure 2.1   Delicious

of services. Rumors swirled that Yahoo! was about to shutter the service. In December 2010, it was sold to Chad Hurley and Steve Chen, two of the founders of YouTube (Wortham, 2011).

Despite the turbulence behind the scenes, Delicious continues to exist as a bookmarking service. After creating a Delicious account, users install a browser-based **bookmarklet** or browser extension. When users are on a page they want to bookmark, they click the button and are presented with a dialogue allowing them to annotate the page and tag it. Tags are user-generated subject headings designed to help users retrieve the bookmark at a later date and to allow them to organize bookmarks in a meaningful way. Delicious bookmarks are cloud-based, so they can be retrieved by visiting the Delicious website. With bookmarks centrally saved in the cloud, users have the same access to all of their bookmarks across machines and devices (the Delicious site is available from any web-enabled device; there is also a Delicious bookmarklet for iOS and third-party Delicious **clients** for Android).

Mobile devices are a space where a bookmarking service can be very convenient. Many users are not in the habit of bookmarking links, as it is often convenient enough to rediscover a link from a desktop computer. Email messages can be searched and search engines can be used until the right link is eventually discovered. But on a mobile device, where bandwidth might be a concern, where connectivity could be inconsistent, and where typing is not always easy, users might want a more direct path to the bookmarks they need. A bookmarking service like Delicious allows users to navigate to a single site and find the bookmark needed, either by tag or by keyword searching captured bookmarks.

Delicious has a relatively new feature called Stacks. This feature allows users to create a page of curated links and images around a single topic. The page can be public or private and other users can be invited to contribute. Users gathering web-based material around a certain topic might see value in making their research publicly available in an easily digestible, annotated way, which is where something like Stacks might come in handy. Sharing content is also discussed in Chapter 8.

Delicious is a simple way to keep track of research found online. But given its volatile history, there are some concerns about its long-term viability as a service. However, Delicious allows users to export their links as a simple HTML file, with users having the option of including their notes and tags, meaning if a user spent a lot of time gathering, tagging, and annotating links, they would still have access to their work as long as they had exported the backup file.

Like many of the services discussed in this book, Delicious has a social component where users can follow other users, seeing what others are bookmarking. Users can also configure Delicious to automatically save links sent from a user's Twitter account. Delicious is a free-of-charge service.

Pinboard

Pinboard (*www.pinboard.in*) is another bookmarking site Figure 2.2). It positions itself as a more robust, viable form of the Delicious service (Pinboard, n.d.). Pinboard does everything Delicious does, except for allowing users to create Stacks. This makes sense, as Pinboard bills itself as "social bookmarking for introverts." That description is not quite fair, though, as, like Delicious, Pinboard does have a social component that allows users to follow other users, seeing what bookmarks they have made publicly available.

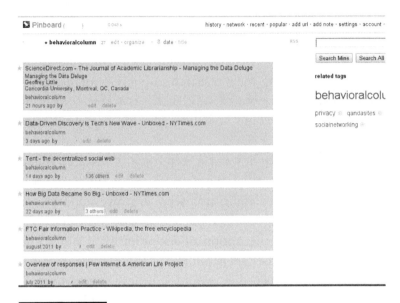

Figure 2.2 Pinboard

Like Delicious, Pinboard also allows users to hook into other social networks and services. In the case of Pinboard, there are quite a few options. Users can configure Pinboard to autopost links from Instapaper, Readability, and Pocket (Pinboard also has its own *Read later* option, see "Postponed reading services" later in this chapter), and even Delicious. That means pages captured using those services will be simultaneously and automatically captured by Pinboard. Like Delicious, Pinboard will also grab links posted on up to three Twitter accounts (like Delicious, the user must own the Twitter accounts). This allows users to make Pinboard a hub for all of their online bookmarking, without even necessarily using Pinboard to natively capture content. This allows users to play with disparate capture services without worrying about having to eventually unify what is being captured. As long as a user is working with a supported service, Pinboard should capture the content. Pinboard also allows users to email links to Pinboard, using a custom email address.

Like Delicious, Pinboard allows users to export their bookmarks as an HTML file. Pinboard also supports bookmark exports into **XML** and **JSON**, which are both flexible data formats.

There is no official Pinboard mobile client, although there are third-party clients available for mobile devices. Pinboard also has a mobile interface available at *m.pinboard.in*.

Pinboard is not a free service. There is a one-time fee to join the service that is based on the number of members. As more people join the service, the fee increases. As of this writing, it is just over $10 to join. Users can also purchase an archiving service from Pinboard, where Pinboard will download a copy of every web page a user bookmarks, allowing them to search archived versions of pages they have captured.

Diigo

Like Pinboard and Delicious, Diigo (*www.diigo.com*) is another bookmarking service (Figure 2.3). In addition to standard bookmarking service features, Diigo allows users to highlight text, capture screen grabs and archive versions of web pages. Like Pinboard and Delicious, Diigo has a browser-based bookmarklet; however, there are also Diigo toolbars for Internet Explorer and Firefox as well as a Chrome extension.

In addition to giving users a Notes field when they initially save a bookmark, Diigo also allows users to add sticky notes to pages they have bookmarked, giving them another way to annotate a page. These notes are visible within the web page

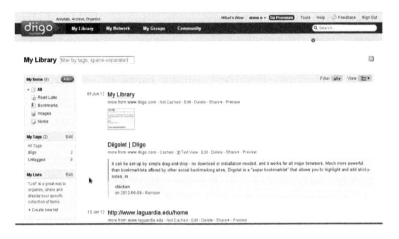

Figure 2.3   Diigo

as long as the user is working with the Diigo toolbar. Otherwise, the notes show up within the web interface, but not tied to specific pieces of text.

Users can also share these notes and annotations with other Diigo users, or can choose to keep certain notes private. Diigo also allows users to create groups, so users can easily share content captured within Diigo.

Users interested in simply capturing bookmarks they wish to return to later would probably be well-served by something simple like Pinboard or Delicious, although Diigo is perfectly effective for this sort of usage, too.

Where Diigo becomes useful is when users need to not only capture pages, but to work with parts of them, marking things up, either for themselves or for others. This sort of markup is trivial to accomplish with paper and pencil, or even with PDFs, but it can be challenging to do with web-based works.

For instance, users working with material from a digital archive might want to use the highlight feature to mark the areas they find to be important or significant. The ability to save local copies of the page means users always have a backup of the site, even if the site is not available. The ability to annotate an electronic version of the page could also prove valuable to users collaborating on a project, as long as both are willing to install the Diigo toolbar. Diigo does not interface with other services the same way Pinboard does, but that is because it's more of a self-contained service. However, Diigo does have some interesting components, such as the ability for Diigo bookmarks to be cross-posted to Delicious. Diigo can also be configured to post bookmarks and annotations as blog posts for users wishing to share what they discover. Diigo also has a communication mechanism within it, so users can send messages to other Diigo users.

There are also Diigo clients for Android and iOS. Diigo is a free service with premium tiers. The premium service includes more space for archived pages and screenshots. Diigo also offers an educator's plan that is free of charge and has more functionality than the default free plan.

Browser bookmark syncing

Tools such as Diigo, Delicious, and Pinboard are useful because of how they let users tag and annotate their bookmarks, giving researchers a few ways to retrieve links they might need at a future date. But for some users, that functionality is overkill. Some users have no desire to catalog their bookmarks – they merely want to use the bookmark toolbar on their browser of choice, but want their bookmarks synced across their various computers.

Certain web browsers now have browser syncing as a built-in option requiring no special downloading or installation. For instance, the Chrome browser allows users to sign into the browser using their Google credential. They can then sign into any Chrome browser and have access to their bookmarks, providing a seamless experience between browsers. The Chrome sign-in credential also syncs browser history, installed extensions, and browser preferences. The sign-in option is under the Chrome customization button (next to the address bar).

Firefox has a similar feature called Firefox sync. It requires the creation of a special Firefox sync account, but once an account is created, like the Chrome sign-in, users can have bookmarks and browser history synced across computers.

Firefox Sync and the Chrome credential work across operating systems.

The Safari browser also allows users to sync their bookmarks via the iCloud service, using their Apple ID as the credential. Safari bookmarks can be synced not only against computers, but also against iOS devices. Safari is available for OS X and Windows, but not Linux.

One limitation of these servers is that they only sync bookmarks at the browser level. Anyone using the built-in Chrome sync feature will have their bookmarks synced across Chrome browsers. But if a user uses multiple browsers, the bookmarks from another browser, such as Internet Explorer will not be synced. Also, if a researcher uses one kind of browser at home and another at work, the bookmarks will not be synced.

A related limitation of these built-in services is that they are not a given for mobile devices. Firefox and Chrome are both available for Android devices, but using a non-default browser on Android devices can be challenging. Interestingly, even though Android is a Google product that uses a Google credential to pull down a lot of user data and preferences, browser bookmarks are not a part of the data sync.

For iPad and iPhone users, there is a Firefox Home app that gives users access to their Firefox history and bookmarks. There is also now a version of Chrome for iOS devices. Conversely, iCloud is an iOS tool, leaving Android users unable to access their Safari bookmarks from their devices.

For users looking for cross-browser bookmark syncing that uses the browser bookmarking feature, another option is Xmarks (*xmarks.com/*). Xmarks is installed in various web browsers, allowing bookmarks to be synced across computers, across web browsers, and across operating systems. The only caveat is that the software needs to be installed in every browser the user wishes to sync. Xmarks is also not available for every browser and operating system combination. For instance, there is no Xmarks for Safari on Windows, although there is one for Safari on OS X. Xmarks also has a web interface, in case a user is on a computer without the Xmarks software installed.

Xmarks is free-of-charge. The free tier includes access to syncing clients for Firefox, Internet Explorer, Chrome and Safari, with Internet Explorer only available for Windows computers and Safari only available for OS X. The premium tier, which is $12 per year, includes access to a variety of mobile clients for iOS, Android, BlackBerry, and others. It also includes a backup service and elevated technical support privileges.

Evernote

Evernote (*www.evernote.com*) is client-based software that takes Diigo a step further, allowing users to not only capture and annotate pages, but also to use the client to construct standalone notes and notebooks (Figure 2.4). In fact, Evernote is perfectly usable without ever using it as a

Figure 2.4   Evernote

bookmark tool. Its strength lies in its ability to be a centralized clearing-house for anything a user might find online and want to save.

Like Diigo, users can choose to capture text, images, or the web page itself. But unlike Diigo, Evernote has a robust note-taking area, allowing users to compose within the text editor, which has a simple word processor-style interface. Some users, especially those working with a lot of web-native content, might even choose to compose work within Evernote, although Evernote only allows users to export in HTML, **.mht** (a web archive format), or Evernote's proprietary format, but not Word or Rich Text Format (**.rtf**).

Evernote allows users to create to-do lists, making it an organizational tool (see Chapter 6). Users can also upload files into Evernote, making it a limited storage tool. In fact, one of the challenges of Evernote is its flexibility. It does so many things so well, it can be challenging to know where to begin.

Users interested in working with Evernote might start small, using it to bookmark and annotate web content. Evernote is rooted in a note/notebook metaphor. Users have the ability to place content into different "notebooks," or sections, within Evernote, and add notes, which can be text, images, and/or bookmarks. This process simulates the process of composing a book or article, with users creating sections in notebooks, just as they are creating sections in an academic work. Users can also tag notes, allowing content to be organized across notebooks. To get started, the user can simply place the annotated bookmark in a notebook and perhaps tag the link. In terms of a research flow, the user could use Evernote to develop a research project, stringing together parts of various smaller works within Evernote notebooks and notes, joining them to create a larger work. This is the strength of Evernote – it is a capture tool that can also evolve into a composition one. The case could even be made that a tool like Evernote is more appropriate to Chapter 5, which discusses composition tools. What makes Evernote a challenging composition tool, though, is there no easy way to export information out of Evernote and into a word processor. Users can email notes and notebooks and can export them as HTML files, but those options all might require some reformatting. Still, for some, it is a small price to pay for access to notes and research across machines and devices.

Although Evernote is client-based, it does have a highly functional web interface. There are also browser extensions for Chrome and Firefox, and a brower-based bookmarklet. Evernote also has clients for a variety of mobile operating systems. In addition to that, there are many tools and services that will work with Evernote, for tasks ranging from a document scanner to handwriting recognition software. These tools work on top of Evernote, either using a user's Evernote data or creating data to be imported directly into Evernote. Users can see the range of services available by visiting the Evernote Trunk (*www.evernote.com/trunk*).

Evernote is available for OS X and Windows but not for Linux, although the Chrome and Firefox extensions are fully cross-platform. However, there is NixNote (*nevernote. sourceforge.net/*), a third-party Evernote clone that is designed to work with Evernote as a Linux client, but that is unsupported and unofficial.

Evernote is free but, like many of the services discussed in this chapter, has a premium tier, which offers features such as additional space, collaboration tools, and offline access.

Springpad

Springpad (*www.springpad.com*) is similar to Evernote, but is entirely web-based (Figure 2.5). Like many of the tools in this chapter, it has a browser bookmarklet and extensions for Firefox and Chrome. The extensions provide a bit more functionality, such as the ability to search through what one has captured. Like Evernote, Springpad uses a notebook concept to help users organize material.

Figure 2.5   Springpad

Springpad uses the term *clip* to refer to bookmarking a page and confusingly calls bookmarks *springs*. Bookmarks can be placed into notebooks as a way of organizing bookmarks and notes. Users can also tag notes within notebooks, as within Evernote. In addition to capturing the URL, Springpad also imports some metadata, such as Universal Product Code (UPC) numbers and pricing.

In addition to URLs, Springpad also allows users to add tasks and checklists, making it an organization tool (see Chapter 6). Users can also upload files, photos, and videos. Springpad has an interesting ability to add material by format, so users looking to add a book to their Springpad can use an internal Springpad search to look for it. If Springpad finds a match, users can add it to their account and a book record will be imported. Springpad also allows users to choose the format of an item when they're saving it into Springpad.

In a similar vein, users can upload content by barcode via the Springpad mobile client, available for both iOS and Android.

Springpad has a social component, where users can follow other users and be followed. It also integrates with networks and services such as Google (contacts and calendar), Twitter, and Facebook. Springpad, unlike Evernote, has a substantial public component, where users can publicly share notebooks as curated content. This is interesting because it means a user's personal research notes could eventually be made public as a resource for others. In general, Springpad has a visual aesthetic, grabbing images by default and using images to represent notebooks and links. It makes for an interesting presentation of information that users might want to use to share their work (see Chapter 8). Users can also collaborate with selected Springpad users on notebooks, which could be an interesting way to conduct a research project.

Springpad is a free service. As far as services go, it is challenging to describe because it does so many things, much like Evernote. Also like Evernote, it is not easy to export data out of Springpad. In fact, it is even harder than Evernote. Where Evernote gives users a notebook and note-level ability to export information, users can only export their entire Springpad collection in one HTML file. On the one hand, it is commendable that Springpad allows data to be exported. But for users to repurpose their data, especially in terms of moving it into some kind of word processor, it could represent a lot of time and effort to shape their Springpad work into something more academic. Still, the immersiveness of Springpad makes it an intriguing capture tool, especially for users with a visual orientation.

Postponed reading services

Web capture can be divided into concepts. One concept is to use the capture as an archive, with a permanent record of whatever web-based object a user was working with, that they wanted to retain. Even if the page itself is not permanent, the link still serves as a reminder of where the information once was. The flip side to archiving exists for users who are not interested in permanently working with a page, but just want to capture the URL long enough to return to the web page. In this instance, users are just looking for a quick place to park a web address until they can return to it later, at a more convenient time. Postponed reading services allow users to bookmark a page, with the idea of returning to it at a later date, but without necessarily using the service to permanently archive and organize bookmarks. Instead, these sites are the web equivalent of a night stand, where users might pile their books to be read at a later date.

As mentioned earlier, Diigo and Pinboard both support this kind of functionality, but there are also dedicated services. Instapaper (*www.instapaper.com*), Readability (*www.readability.com*), and Pocket (*www.getpocket.com*) (Figure 2.6) are examples of this kind of service. Facebook, the social network, also now gives users the ability to save certain content for later viewing.

These services all have a bookmarklet that allow users to capture what they wish to read later. The workflow for all three services is the same. The user visits a page but does not have time to read it or explore it, so the user bookmarks it in one of these services and then accesses the pages at a later date using the service chosen. For instance, a user might capture a web page using the Instapaper service. The next time they visit their Instapaper page, they will be presented with a list of everything they have bookmarked, including that page. Where these postponed reading services become useful is in access. Each of these services has a mobile application allowing a user to access their reading list on a

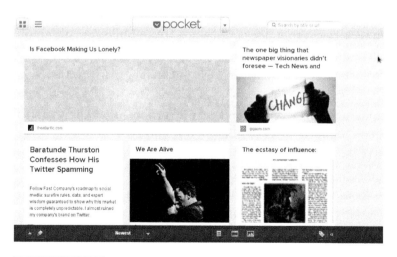

Figure 2.6 Pocket

tablet or mobile device. So users just need to remember to check their reading lists on these services at regular intervals. Each of the services also saves a local copy of the web page, meaning users do not need Internet access to read the content, so long as the device has synced with the service. The local copy of the web page is also formatted for easier reading, which is helpful for users on devices with small screens, such as smart phones. These services will extract text and images from a web page and present it on a plain white background, without any advertisements. The presentation of the content is one of the things that these postponement services do successfully that more fully featured bookmark services, such as Pinboard, Delicious, and Diigo, simply do not do as well. Postponed reading services, for the most part, do one thing, but they do that one thing very well.

In terms of services, Instapaper, Pocket, and Readability are all very similar. Instapaper's interface is the sparsest, but it is also the only one that allows users to organize their reading list into folders, which some might feel is not truly in the spirit of these sorts of services, which are about reading and not organizing. Instapaper is also the only of these services that does not have a free mobile app, although there are some third-party tools that provide mobile access to Instapaper content for free. Instapaper also allows users to link their Instapaper account to social networks, bookmarking services, and even Evernote, allowing them to share what they are reading. Users can also send Instapaper articles to their Kindle. Instapaper has a free tier and a subscription tier with more functionality.

Readability's interface is a bit nicer than Instapaper's, as it presents the opening sentence along with the article title. It also provides some ability to socially share reading. Like Instapaper, Readability provides a private email address users can use to email links to their reading list.

Pocket arguably has the nicest interface, with the web interface presenting articles represented by images from the articles, making the page look like a news site.

OneNote

OneNote is another capture tool (Figure 2.7). It is a part of the Microsoft Office suite and is only available for PCs. OneNote 2010 is more easily cloud syncable than the 2007 edition, which does not directly integrate with Windows Live SkyDrive (*skydrive.live.com*), Microsoft's web-based file storage product (see Chapter 4). OneNote is client based, allowing users to quickly grab images, record audio and jot down ideas, with the OneNote environment providing tools, such as tabs, tags, notebooks, and a search feature, to allow the user to assemble the detritus into a usable document. In that sense, it is similar to Evernote, although

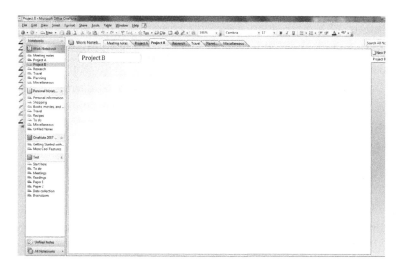

Figure 2.7 OneNote

depending upon the version of OneNote being used, it is not nearly as syncable. OneNote notes can be maintained in a side window of the client, with notes later organized in a more robust client view (OneNote, like many of the products discussed in this chapter, uses a notes/notebook metaphor for users to organize their work). This allows users to grab content as they work, without necessarily having to launch the full OneNote client and then add content to a new window.

With all of these limitations, why would anyone choose OneNote? The main reason would be its integration with Microsoft products and services, from the Outlook email client to Word, to the SharePoint server technology. OneNote allows a user to seamlessly integrate these tools with little risk of any formatting being lost in translation. That means a user could use OneNote to gather all of their notes around a project, shape the notes into a draft document and then export the work directly into Word, where all OneNote formatting would remain. For users trying to avoid the Google ecosystem, OneNote can also represent another option, although, as mentioned earlier, OneNote syncability ease depends upon the version being used. Still, many people are enthusiastic about OneNote's potential (Dawson, 2010).

OneNote has some collaboration features, allowing users to share notebooks. Content can also be emailed out of OneNote so that users without OneNote can still view content, even if they cannot edit it themselves. OneNote also has a number of templates to help users set up their OneNote notebooks.

OneNote is not free but as part of the Microsoft Office suite it is commonly available at many institutions. A lot of institutions also provide home access to the Office suite. There is also a OneNote app for Windows Phone 8, iOS, and Android.

Conclusion

Choosing a web capture tool is not easy because of all of the tools and options available to users. The first thing researchers should consider is what they want to capture. Those only interested in scholarly content might be better served by some of the tools described in Chapter 3, which provide citation options. But many, if not all, of the tools in this chapter can be used to manage academic work, although it might require some work on the part of the user. For instance, users capturing scholarly web content via a tool like Pinboard would have to make sure they have proxy information included in the bookmarked URLs, otherwise off-campus access might be an issue. But, in general, if a user just wants to capture URLs with some kind of brief tagging or annotation, Delicious or Pinboard should be more than sufficient. For users who are not even interested in annotations, one of the browser bookmark syncing services might be sufficient. While browser bookmarks do not support tagging, they do allow users to place bookmarks within folders, which can be considered a type of subject-level organization.

Some users might want something a bit more robust, though; they might want something that not only captures URLs, but also provides a way for the user to give context to the captured site. This is where something like Diigo comes in. Its ability to annotate pages makes it useful for capturing not just addresses, but a user's notes and ideas about the pages – even giving users the ability to annotate on the page itself.

For users looking for something that captures web content, but also allows users to organize words and ideas (and also images, to a certain extent), something like Springpad or Evernote might be worth exploring. These tools are versatile, making them difficult to describe and to categorize, but that versatility is what makes them so flexible. On the one hand, there is more of a learning curve for these kinds of tools, because they are relatively complex. But the payoff for that complexity is a robust tool that allows users to access notes and research from anywhere they have web access. An added benefit is that many users will also find these capture tools useful for composition and/or organization, allowing them to accomplish many tasks in one tool. For instance, the notebook structure of Evernote allows users to grow a work in sections, very organically.

Users should be cautioned against tying up too much information, especially important research around projects, in a proprietary tool. Tools like Evernote and Springpad are versatile and allow users to export their data, but depending upon the complexity of a user's setup, making sense out of what was exported might become a time-consuming process. This is not to say that users should not become invested in these tools. It is merely a reminder of the importance of backing up data and making sure there is a contingency plan for retrieving it should something go wrong with a product or service. It could be something as simple as cross-posting bookmarks to another service, so a user always has a backup of their saved URLs, if not their complete notes. Or it could simply be regular exports of all data, with the user hoping they never have to go through everything outside the service to reconstruct their research.

3

Capturing and managing scholarly information

Abstract: Bibliographic management tools allow users to save and organize citations (and sometimes the full-text of articles), while also providing the option to export citations in different citation formats. Cloud-based tools are no different, but provide the added advantage of persistent access to this information across computers and devices. This chapter will discuss pure cloud-based tools, such as CiteULike, RefWorks, and the organizational tools within subscription databases. Client-based tools that can be synced against the cloud, such as Zotero, Mendeley, EndNote, and Papers will also be discussed, as will BibTeX, a markup-driven method to manage citations. When choosing a service, users should focus on cost, the operating systems of their computers and mobile devices, their commonly used citation formats, and the interface of the tools. Luckily, it is usually not difficult to export citations out of one bibliographic management tool and into another, so users can easily experiment with multiple tools.

Key words: bibliographic management, BibTeX, citation management, citations, CiteULike, EndNote, Mendeley, Papers, RefWorks, Zotero.

Research is all about finding what is needed to answer a question. For most academic researchers, that means books and articles. But with more and more information available electronically, books and articles don't necessarily mean physical resources. For many researchers, contemporary research takes place on a screen, with material pulled in from subscription databases, online archives, and electronic books.

While Chapter 2 discussed capturing and organizing information found online from non-scholarly materials, this chapter will discuss how to effectively capture scholarly online material. The separation is necessary because the capture and organization of scholarly and non-scholarly material can involve different processes.

Scholarly web-based material tends to have more metadata than non-scholarly material and the metadata tends to be structured in a standardized way that allows tools, like the ones that will be discussed in this chapter, to extract it in a meaningful way for the end-user. For instance, scholarly metadata might include things like the publication title, the place of publication, author information, and publication date. Those items are hardly a given on a general web page.

For instance, that structured metadata can be used to easily create bibliographies or instantly organize a list of works by publication date or author. That level of organization is not possible with many of the non-scholarly materials users encounter online. To be fair, that level of organization also is often not required for those kinds of materials.

The tools discussed in this chapter are a conceptual subset of the tools discussed in Chapter 2. The tools discussed in Chapter 2 could certainly be used for scholarly capture, but users would miss out on a lot of helpful functionality available via the tools discussed here.

How do researchers keep track of scholarly research?

For many, the answer is a hard copy that the user prints. Print is convenient. Users can write on it. Users can easily carry it with them; they can see the print in neat little piles all over the office. However, as nice and convenient as print is, it also has its challenges. For instance, what happens if a print article is lost? Will users be able to retrace their steps to find it again?

For some, an even more daunting thought is citing everything they have found. Many researchers are familiar with the citation style of their discipline, but some journals and publishers use citation styles that are unfamiliar to users. While learning a new citation style is hardly rocket science, very few people relish the thought of converting citations to a new format.

Luckily, there are tools that help researchers organize scholarly work. These bibliographic management tools allow users to not only keep track of their citations, but also to export their citations into specific citation styles. These cloud-based (or cloud-syncable) tools are available from any computer with Internet access, meaning not only does a researcher have constant access to their citations, but also that, should anything happen to a main work computer, there is always a backup of the citations being used.

RefWorks

Unlike the purely cloud-based tools discussed in this chapter, RefWorks (*www.refworks.com*) does not have a free tier (Figure 3.1). As of this writing it costs $100 a year for a

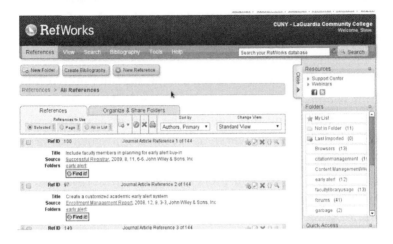

Figure 3.1 RefWorks

personal subscription. However, many academic libraries subscribe to RefWorks, making it free to any user associated with the subscribing institution. RefWorks also allows alumni to maintain access to RefWorks, meaning if a user leaves an institution, their saved RefWorks citations will be able to go with them.

RefWorks tracks citations for users, allowing them to import material as they encounter it. While it's obviously optimized for electronic-based research, users can also manually import citations from print sources. In addition to acting as a database for citations, RefWorks, like all of the tools discussed in this chapter, allows users to export their citations in a variety of citation formats, so a list of imported citations can easily be converted to any number of formats.

Because RefWorks is so common in academic settings, many scholarly resources provide an option to export citations directly into RefWorks. You'll see the option within subscription collections such as ScienceDirect, the EBSCOHost platform, and even within Google Scholar (the option is under *Scholar Preferences*). The user selects the articles they wish to retain, logs into RefWorks, and then exports their data into RefWorks. With the data within RefWorks, the user can now manipulate and organize it however they see fit, putting articles into virtual folders, or adding additional metadata, including notes.

In addition to exporting citations out of tools into RefWorks, RefWorks also has a browser bookmarklet, Firefox add-on, and Internet Explorer plugin, all called RefGrab-It, that lets users import the metadata from articles they find online. Users find a book or article online, click a browser button and RefWorks imports the page, figuring out whatever metadata it can. It's not a perfect system, but when it works, it's tremendously helpful, in that you do not need to manually key in data.

RefWorks also integrates with openURL services, such as SFX or SerialsSolutions 360 link. OpenURL services allow institutions, almost always libraries, to automatically connect a user to full text when the full text of an article is not available in the collection the user is searching. OpenURL services track holdings and direct users to where in a library's electronic holdings the full text of an article (or book) can be found. RefWorks is a bibliographic management tool and not a content collection, so it does not have the full text of any article. But if a library has configured RefWorks to work with an openURL service, users will see links within RefWorks that will take them to the full text of an article. This can be a helpful functionality if a user has misplaced an article and wants to quickly access it again. For researchers who don't want to leave anything to chance, RefWorks also allows users to upload files to citation records, meaning that if an article is no longer electronically available online, the user will always have their locally saved copy attached to their RefWorks citation. This is a standard feature for

RefWorks' institutional licenses but is an add-on to a personal one.

It is easy to see how helpful this functionality is and if all RefWorks did was manage citations, it would probably be a worthy time investment. But where RefWorks really shines is in its ability to generate citations in a specific format. Users can easily generate a bibliography by selecting the citations they wish to export and choosing a citation format. RefWorks has hundreds of citation formats in its database and allows users to create custom output formats if a format is not already in the RefWorks system. Citations will often need to be tweaked, but using RefWorks gives users a place to start their bibliographies without creating one from scratch.

RefWorks also offers a feature called Write-N-Cite that allows it to integrate with Microsoft Word, inserting citations from RefWorks as the user composes in Word. The citations are temporary until the user indicates the paper is finished. Then, the citations and formatting are locked into the paper in a finalized version of the original document. This is helpful, because citations can change as a work evolves. Write-N-Cite allows for that kind of flexibility.

RefWorks also has a mobile interface allowing users to access their citations from mobile devices, as well as add them. As you might expect, the mobile version of the RefWorks website is not as full-featured as the standard one. For instance, there is no openURL integration in the mobile version. Also, the full site does not redirect users to the mobile version. Users must know the web address for the RefWorks mobile interface (*www.refworks.com/mobile*).

Some institutions might also subscribe to RefShare, which allows users to share citations with each other, either at an institutional level, or beyond.

Finally, RefWorks allows users to export their citations in a variety of bibliographic management formats, and as a simple tag delimited file, so if a user decides RefWorks is not for them, they can pull their data out, perhaps even importing it into another bibliographic management tool.

Mendeley

Mendeley (*www.mendeley.com*) has been called the iTunes of scholarly research (Chivers, 2011), which makes sense – it's a desktop client that allows users to organize and access scholarly papers the same way iTunes allows user to organize and access music and video (Figure 3.2).

The simplicity of both tools is also comparable. Just as users can easily drag multimedia into iTunes, researchers can easily drag scholarly content into Mendeley. Mendeley will then interpret the metadata and import that into the client.

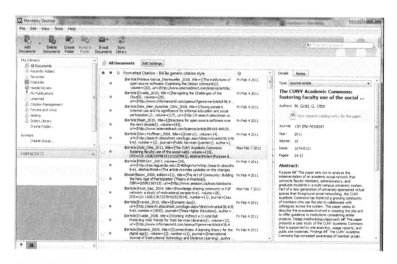

Figure 3.2   Mendeley

For instance, if a researcher has a **PDF** from a journal, they merely need to import the file into Mendeley and Mendeley will use the document metadata to determine bibliographic variables such as the author, article title, and publication date. Of course, for articles where that metadata is not present (a very real possibility when researchers find articles in self-posted faculty collections via Google and not via subscription tools, where metadata is more the norm), Mendeley will not be able to determine bibliographic information on its own.

While Mendeley is a desktop client, with clients for Windows, OS X, and Linux, its strength lies is in its ability to sync against a cloud-based server. Users can sync their Mendeley library against the cloud, giving them web-based access to their files and citations. Mendeley also supports the use of multiple synced clients, so users can have the Mendeley client installed across devices and machines, with the same content available in each instance.

The Mendeley client does many helpful things for users. It can monitor certain desktop folders for content and automatically import it. That means a user's research process could be as simple as downloading PDFs into those watched folders and automatically seeing those PDFs within the Mendeley interfaces.

The client will also format citations into a bibliographic style, allowing users to quickly copy cited articles and paste them into a bibliography. Mendeley installs with a few citation styles by default, but allows users to import other styles. Users can also create their own citation format, which involves some XML editing (Ridout, 2011).

While the Mendeley client is very useful, it is just one aspect of what makes Mendeley so powerful. Another, complementary component, is what Mendeley calls the Web Importer, a web-browser-based bookmark, comparable to

RefWorks' RefGrab-It feature. The Mendeley Web Importer is configured to work with a number of database products, such as EBSCOHost, JSTOR, and Elseivier's ScienceDirect, but also with free services, such as Amazon, Google Books, and Google Scholar. The Web Importer allows users to import article or book metadata from a browser and import it into Mendeley, where the data will eventually be synced with the client.

For users who don't want to use the client, the Mendeley web interface is quite robust, giving users access to all of their saved articles, including any PDFs they've associated with their account (and that they've chosen to sync). However, the web interface does not allow citations to be exported in specific formats.

Many researchers will find Mendeley very useful as a standalone tool, but it has some collaborative and social features that can also be helpful. For instance, users can create groups, which allow members to share books and articles with each other, a collaborative bibliography of sorts. Groups can be private or public. Private groups can also share full-text documents with each other, saving individual group members the trouble of tracking down the full text of shared citations.

Mendeley also acts as an impressive, if slightly random, search tool, allowing users to search through everything captured within Mendeley by all of its users. There is also a browsing feature with papers arranged by discipline. The randomness comes from the fact that Mendeley searches only what has been captured, but not everything that exists. As a result, significant runs of important journals could be missing because they have not yet been saved within Mendeley.

Interestingly, when browsing, users can import citations found through the Mendeley search, or they can download

PDFs, if the PDF is publicly available, as is the case with many items found via tools such as PubMed. Available PDFs can be downloaded right into the client via the web interface, without the user needing to save the file into a watched folder, or manually import a document.

Users can also connect with each other, allowing them to share their work and discover users with similar research interests.

One of the interesting things about Mendeley is that it offers some degree of integration with Zotero, so if there are aspects of some, or both, of those tools that a user wants, it's viable to use multiple tools, without having duplicate citations and having to add citations multiple times.

To share Zotero citations with Mendeley, users need to direct their Mendeley client to their Zotero database via the options menu. Once the Zotero database is imported, Mendely will automatically add Zotero citations that are added to the local database. That means the Mendeley citations will be up-to-date with Zotero citations, as long as the local Zotero instance is synced.

CiteULike, Zotero, and RefWorks allow users to import citations but do not have an automatic sync with any of the other services discussed here.

Mendeley has a free tier, with additional space and functionality (related to the number of private groups and group members) available for a monthly fee. There is also an iOS Mendeley app. Mendeley has an institutional edition for schools, which provides additional functionality, such as better integration of local electronic resources. Mendeley has plugins for Word and OpenOffice/LibreOffice/NeoOffice, allowing users to import citations and bibliographies.

Zotero

Zotero (*www.zotero.org*) is another bibliographic management tool (Figure 3.3). It started as an advanced Firefox add-on, meaning users who wished to use Zotero had to use the Firefox browser. However, there is also now a standalone client for Windows, OS X, and Linux.

Like Mendeley and RefWorks, Zotero is designed to capture and organize web-based research. The standalone client is not yet as developed as Mendeley. For instance, the Zotero standalone client does not import metadata out of PDFs the way the Mendeley client can by default. Instead, users must download an add-on to make that feature possible.

However, the Firefox add-on version of Zotero is quite useful, with a lot of features that make it very simple to import and organize data. For instance, as a user surfs the web, Zotero will display icons in the address bar indicating it has detected a format it recognizes. A user searching a library catalog might come across a book that looks interesting. Conveniently, Zotero recognizes that this is a book record and displays a book icon in the address bar. Clicking the book imports the book metadata into Zotero, where it can be organized into folders and/or given notes and

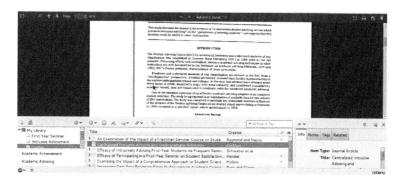

Figure 3.3   Zotero

tags. The same process applies to other formats, including videos. Zotero can also save archives of web pages, creating a locally saved version of a web page, which might come in handy if a page suddenly disappears from the Internet, or in a situation where there is limited Internet connectivity.

Zotero, like Mendeley, supports syncing across devices, so users can keep their citations aligned across computers. There is also a web interface for when a user is on a machine without the client or the Firefox add-on. Users can also manually add citations through the web interface. There is no bookmarklet, like RefWorks' RefGrab-It or Mendeley's Web Importer, but there are plugins for Google Chrome and Safari. Users of other browsers might face more challenges importing web-based content on the fly.

Another tremendously helpful Zotero feature is its proxy detection and redirection. Library proxies are used to authenticate users from off-campus. They allow users to sign-in with a credential, and, upon verification of the credential, be passed along to the subscription-based site. One of the challenges of proxies, though, is that the user needs to understand them to a certain extent. If a user is searching a service such as JSTOR from off-campus via a library website, the proxy information should automatically be provided and they should have a seamless browsing experience. However, if the user encounters a JSTOR link away from a library site, perhaps via Google Scholar, for example, the user might not have off-campus access to the article if there is no proxy to authenticate them into JSTOR. They would need to know to manually provide the proxy information. Zotero tries to make this process easier by offering to remember proxy information for users, adding it into URLs when Zotero detects a proxy can be used. Zotero can also remember multiple proxy configurations for users who might have multiple affiliations, with multiple subscription options. The proxy configuration options only seem to be available via the Firefox add-on and not within the standalone client. However, it is worth noting that the client supports openURL resolvers, much like RefWorks does, although configuring this could be very challenging. Many libraries are providing setup guides to help their users configure this option. Once configured, users can use the Zotero library lookup option to see if their institution provides electronic access to an article in their Zotero library.

The Zotero client also has an impressive ability to import metadata when a user provides an **ISBN, DOI,** or **PMID.** Zotero uses that information to look up the item metadata and import it.

Zotero, like Mendeley, has word processing plugins for LibreOffice/OpenOffice/NeoOffice, as well as Microsoft Word. Zotero does not have an official mobile client, but there are some third-party clients designed to integrate with Zotero.

Like Mendeley, Zotero allows users to create public and private groups, with a group library of shared citations. While the web interface allows Zotero users to browse group content, when using the Firefox add-on or standalone client they can easily drag and drop group documents into their own Zotero holdings. Users can also follow each other, to facilitate professional communication.

Zotero is free with additional storage available for a monthly fee.

CiteULike

CiteULike (*www.citeulike.org*) is an entirely web-based bibliographic manager, and perhaps the simplest of the ones discussed so far (Figure 3.4). Its simplicity is, however, a feature.

Figure 3.4   CiteULike

Like RefWorks and Mendeley, there is a browser-based bookmark that allows users to import content they encounter. They can also export citations in a format such as **BibTeX** or the commonly used **RIS** citation format and then import the ciations into CiteULike.

Despite the lack of a client, users can still accomplish most of what they can using any of the other tools discussed. They can attach files to their records, associating PDFs with article citations, and they can organize their files using tags. CiteULike also offers some rating functionality, if users wish to rate their articles or eventually sort a list of articles by rating.

Like Mendeley, users can search the entire CiteULike database and copy citations into their own article listings. Like the other tools discussed, CiteULike lets users export citations in a variety of bibliographic formats, although it doesn't offer as many formats as RefWorks, Mendeley, or Zotero on its free tier.

CiteULike has some of the same social features seen in some of the other tools discussed. Users can create public and private groups for sharing citations. They can create watch lists of what other users are adding to CiteULike, compiling a social bibliography. In fact, the CiteULike interface will look familiar to users of the Delicious bookmarking service (see Chapter 2), which is also designed to let users capture information while allowing other users to see what is being captured. CiteULike accomplishes the same thing, but with academic content. CiteULike also lets users connect with each other: if both users agree to a connection, they can send messages to each other and see each other's CiteULike activities on their home page. CiteULike will also recommend articles based upon articles the user has added to their collection.

CiteULike is free, with a paid tier that includes additional functionality, like the ability to annotate PDFs, priority technical support, some customization options, and access to more citation formats.

EndNote

EndNote is probably best known as a citation management client for OS X and Windows (Figure 3.5). However, versions X5 and X6 integrate with EndNote Web, providing cloud-based access to a user's EndNote citations. It should be noted that unlike many of the other products discussed so far in this chapter, EndNote is a for-purchase product retailing for around $250, with a cheaper student version available with the same features as the full version (students have to provide a copy of a current and valid student ID to purchase this). EndNote also offers institutional packages, so interested users might want to investigate whether their campus can provide free access to the installation file. EndNote also allows users to try out the software for 30 days without purchasing it.

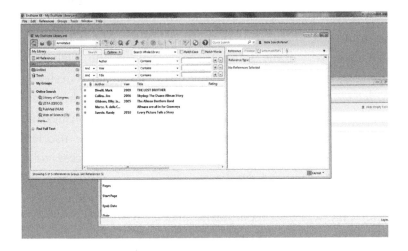

Figure 3.5   EndNote

In addition to being a robust citation manager, EndNote allows users to view and annotate PDFs. It is also possible to search certain web-based collections via the EndNote interface.

EndNote has a toolbar for Firefox and Internet Explorer allowing users to capture citations as they search online. Many subscription tools also support exporting citations specifically for EndNote, although EndNote can easily import RIS-formatted citations. Some non-subscription tools can export into EndNote, including Google Scholar.

EndNote also integrates with Microsoft Word, Apache, OpenOffice, Apple Pages and Mathematica for Windows via a tool called Cite While You Write, which lets users access and insert their EndNote databases into their word processor.

EndNote also has some social functionality, allowing EndNote Web users to collaborate via groups.

EndNote is a powerful and highly configurable tool, but it requires the user to manually sync their locally hosted citations against the web-based version of the tool. If the user forgets to do this regularly, they could easily lose a lot of important data in the event of a hard-drive crash. Also, given its cost, it might be hard to justify purchasing EndNote when there are many free alternatives. However, if price is not an option or if users can obtain EndNote from their institution, it might be worth exploring, as it's a classic piece of software in terms of bibliographic management. Also worth considering is that formal technical support is included with the purchase of EndNote. There is an iPad app for EndNote.

Papers

Papers (*www.papersapp.com/papers/*; Mekentosj, n.d.) is another client-oriented bibliographic management program (Figure 3.6). Once only available for OS X, there is now a Windows client as well. Like EndNote, Papers is not

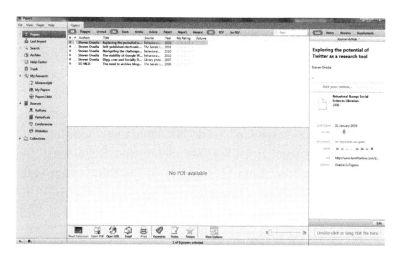

Figure 3.6   Papers

free-of-charge (it retails for $79 and offers a discount for graduate and undergraduate students).

Papers and Mendeley have similar looks, with both interfaces seemingly modeled on iTunes. One interesting component to Papers is that upon logging into the client for the first time, it tries to find works written by the person creating the account, giving the user the option of importing those citations into Papers right away. The search seems to be coming from the WorldCat catalog (*www.worldcat.org*).

Like Zotero, Papers has convenient library proxy support. While Zotero detects proxies, Papers gives users a list of library proxies from which to choose. If a user's institution is not listed, Papers provides instructions on how to get the institutional proxy information added to Papers. Once that proxy information is input and correct, Papers will put subscription links through the user's home library proxy, allowing them off-campus access to material they might not have discovered through the library website. For instance, some of the works imported on creating a Papers account will have links to subscription resources. Papers will put those links through the user's proxy, so if they are entitled to off-campus access to those articles, they will have it.

Users wishing to add material to Papers can simply drag PDFs into the interface. Papers will interpret whatever metadata it can from the documents. Users can also manually add and enhance citations. Users can also add works to Papers via a browser-based bookmarklet. Unlike the bookmarklets for CiteULike, Mendeley, and RefWorks, the Papers browser bookmarklet simply opens the current web page within the Papers interface and then gives the user the option to import the work into Papers. Some users will find this process a bit slower than the one used by the other tools. This is because the user is toggling between two applications to import a citation. Also, the quality of the metadata imported varies depending upon the web page a user is working with. Papers data can always be edited, though.

Like so many of the tools discussed in this chapter, Papers also has a social component. Using the unusually named Papers Livfe function, Papers users can join and create groups called collections. The collections are shared citations that can be briefly annotated and imported into a user's personal Papers collection. Collections can be public or private and are designed to make it easy to facilitate the sharing of citations. To its credit, the Papers interface makes this sharing effortless. Users just right click a citation to share it as a collection. They can also see a running list of their collections on their Papers client. Users just need to click a collection and can immediately begin reviewing shared citations.

Like some of the other tools discussed, Papers can also insert references as users compose in a word processor. For supported word processors, such as Microsoft Word, Papers will insert links to citations and then import and format the citations when the user has finished writing. For unsupported word processors, Papers will still very easily insert a formatted citation, letting the user choose the format style as they select citations, meaning if a user wanted one citation in MLA and another in APA, they could easily import the two citations in two different formats. Paper does this via a very interesting tool called Magic Manuscripts. The user accesses Magic Manuscripts via a key combination and is presented with a search box that is independent of the Papers client. The user types the citation they want and Magic Manuscripts presents matching citations. At this point, the user can also choose the format of a specific citation. While the functionality is most helpful for supported word processors because it will handle in-text citation for the user, it is still quite helpful for unsupported word processors, where it gives users the option to simply import a formatted citation. Papers supports over 1400 citation formats. Any user-generated papers with imported citations will also appear in the Papers interface.

While Papers is very powerful, of all the tools discussed here, it is weakest in terms of syncing data across machines and devices. OS X users have the option of syncing their data via the Papers iOS client. Windows users do not have that option yet, although Papers developers say Windows support is coming soon (Mekentosj B.V., n.d.). However, the lack of a cloud sync puts Papers at a tremendous disadvantage compared to the other tools discussed. Where the other tools allow users to access their citations from any device, Papers users are limited in their access and need to plan accordingly. As an alternative, some users keep their Papers database file in a cloud environment and use that cloud-hosted file as a way to sync Papers across computers, although that method is not officially supported.

Papers can import a variety of citation formats, including RIS and BibTeX. Users can also export their citations out of Papers in a variety of standard citation formats.

Subscription databases

Many subscription databases provide their own citation management functionality (for example EBSCO, Figure 3.7). If a user finder themselves regularly using a single subscription collection, or multiple collections from the same vendor, they might want to investigate whether the product has some sort of built-in citation management tool. The advantage to a built-in tool is the convenience. Users are able to capture citations exactly where they discover them. However, there are also some challenges to these sorts of tools.

Figure 3.7 EBSCO

One significant challenge is that many users draw research from more than one vendor, meaning if a user wishes to capture everything they are using for their research, they'll need at least two citation lists: one for subscription database content and one for everything outside of that particular database.

Access could also present another challenge. Some subscription tools allow users to log in and access their work, even if they no longer have institutional access to the collection, but other tools require a subscription for access. This means if a user changes job or if their institution cancels an electronic subscription, they could be left without access to their citations.

Also, the subscription database citation management tools vary in their functionality and in the range of citation styles they support. For instance, EBSCOhost's citation management tool, which is called My EBSCOhost, allows users to export their sources into another a tool, such as RefWorks, or in a variety of formats, such as RIS and BibTeX, but does not allow them to export multiple citations in one particular citation format. Users must either download the articles along with some of EBSCOhost's citations (MLA, APA, Chicago/Turabian, and a few others) or download one citation at a time from each individual article. While for many, this is still much easier than creating citations from scratch, it is less convenient than the flow for many of the tools discussed within this chapter.

For users interested in exploring these database-housed tools, the first step is to determine whether a database they use frequently has some kind of citation management functionality. EBSCOhost has the My EBSCOhost area. That tool is fairly robust, allowing users to save searches and to organize their research into folders. JSTOR has a MyJSTOR tool that is less robust, basically allowing users to keep a single list of all citations they wish to retain. JSTOR does not allow users to choose a citation format, but, like My EBSCOhost, it does allow users to export their JSTOR data into a third-party tool using common citation formats. ScienceDirect's personalized area is even less robust, merely capturing previous searches and document views, but not allowing users to choose what is (and is not) retained. ProQuest has an interesting compromise, allowing users to use a RefWorks credential to unify their citations, so non-ProQuest citations show up within the ProQuest interface. This is because RefWorks is a ProQuest product. ProQuest does allow some citation management options for users without a RefWorks account.

Users interested in using a subscription database tool to manage their citations might start by seeing whether the collection they wish to use has some sort of ability create an account. Once an account is created, that is usually where the citation management functionality will be found. Users who are still unsure might wish to contact the database vendor or their electronic resources librarian.

BibTeX

It should be noted immediately that BibTeX is not for the faint-hearted (Figure 3.8). BibTeX is a format designed to work with the **LaTeX** markup language/typesetting system. LaTeX was traditionally used by scientists and mathematicians because of its ability to typeset formulas. Many users, even outside those disciplines, use it because of the high degree of control it gives users over the presentation of their documents. BibTeX is a way to manage citations for LaTeX documents. Users insert links to BibTeX citations within their LaTeX document and configure LaTeX to provide a formatted citation. There are also some tools that allow users to use BibTeX with word processors, such as Word, Apache and

```
@string{jgr = "J.~Geophys.~Res."}

@MISC{primes,
    author = "Charles Louis Xavier Joseph de la Vall(\'e}e Poussin",
    note = "A strong form of the prime number theorem, 19th century",
    year = 1879
    }

@INBOOK{chicago,
    title = "The Chicago Manual of Style",
    publisher = "University of Chicago Press",
    edition = "Thirteenth",
    year = 1982,
    pages = "400--401",
    key = "Chicago"
    }

@BOOK{texbook,
    author = "Donald E. Knuth",
    title= "The {{\TeX}book}",
    publisher = "Addison-Wesley",
    year = 1984
    }

@BOOK{latexbook,
    author = "Leslie Lamport",
    title = "{\LaTeX \rm:} {A} Document Preparation System",
    publisher = "Addison-Wesley",
    year = 1986
    }

@UNPUBLISHED{btxdoc,
    author = "Oren Patashnik",
    title = "{Using BibTeX}",
    note = "Documentation for general BibTeX users",
    month = jan
```

Figure 3.8   BibTeX

OpenOffice. All of this requires a fair amount of knowledge and understanding.

While there are a variety of LaTeX editors on all platforms to help users build LaTeX documents, there is still a steep learning curve. BibTeX can also be complicated, although working with it is made easier by the fact that most subscription resources will provide a BibTeX-formatted citation for users. In fact, all of the tools in this chapter can both import and export BibTeX citations. If a user was so inclined, they could keep a BibTeX file of their citations hosted in the cloud and manually add citations as needed. This process would not be as convenient as any of the other tools discussed in this chapter, and could be especially challenging in situations where there is no pre-formatted BibTeX option. The user would either have to build the BibTeX citation by hand or import it into one of the tools discussed above and then export the BibTeX. Many subscription tools, and Google Scholar, allow users to export citations as BibTeX. But for a user who wants a high degree of control over their documents and who enjoys the simplicity of a text file, BibTeX could represent an interesting option.

There are many online resources for both BibTeX and LaTeX. The best place to start for BibTeX background is *www.bibtex.org/*. Users interested in LaTeX should begin with the project home page: *www.latex-project.org/*.

Conclusion

Bibliographic management is a very personal choice. Most of the tools discussed in this chapter have similar features, so for the important issues, like turning a ScienceDirect article citation into an APA formatted one, any of the tools will be fine. Any of these tools will also help users organize their citations and most, with the notable exception of BibTex, provide a way for users to easily collaborate and/or share citations with colleagues.

The issue of which tool to select, then, comes down to a few variables. One important factor will be the user's platform. Papers is most effective for OS X users. Windows users would not have access to all of the same functionality, specifically the ability to sync with an iOS device. Which also brings up the issue of Papers and Android devices, where Android users might be challenged by the lack of a Papers Android client.

Linux users will also have fewer tools to consider. They would not be able to natively work with Papers or EndNote, although committed users could run either in a virtual Windows machine on their Linux system.

Cost is another variable. Many of the tools discussed here are free-of-charge, but Papers is not. Depending upon the user's institutional access, RefWorks and/or EndNote might be free for end-users. Mendeley and Zotero have paid tiers, with monthly charges, although much can be accomplished in the free tiers of those services. Depending upon the reference format needed, users might have to pay for CiteULike.

Collaborators will also be an important variable if a researcher expects to share citations. If everyone working on a project is using a different bibliographic management tool, it could be challenging to share work. So collaborators probably want to agree on which tool they'll use.

Users interested in using a tool to interact with their word processor might want to test some of these tools and determine ease of use. As a general rule, most of these tools seem optimized to work with Microsoft Word, but for users of other word processors, such as LibreOffice or even

Google Drive, a user might have to experiment to find which tool provides the easiest word processing integration.

All things being equal, if a researcher regularly uses Firefox, the Zotero Firefox extension is probably the easiest tool to use (perhaps even easier than the Zotero standalone client). Everything can be easily managed from within the browser and syncing is almost instantaneous. The Zotero Firefox extension is a perfect cross between a client and a bookmarklet. Users can add citations with the same ease as adding a browser bookmark. However, at the same time, Zotero has the robustness of a client, with the ability to quickly manage and export citations. But most conveniently of all, Zotero doesn't require the user to open a client. Instead, all of the management occurs in the Zotero Firefox pane.

A final note to consider is that because there are standardized reference formats, such as BibTeX and RIS, users are rarely locked into one tool. As long as the user chooses a tool that allows easy exporting, which all of the tools mentioned here do allow, they can try different tools without the risk of losing years of data. Although, depending upon the tool, notes and PDF annotations might be lost between systems. But in general, if a user just wants to manage citations and export them in a specific format for bibliographies, and, if they don't mind doing a little bit of data cleanup, moving between bibliographic management tools is a relatively simple task – especially given that so many of the tools provide the ability to interact with each other. For instance, if a user tires of CiteULike or Zotero, they can try Mendeley, which has the ability to easily capture citations from those tools. It is fortunate that data lock-in does not seem to be an issue with bibliographic management tools.

4

Storing files in the cloud

Abstract: Cloud-based file syncing allows users convenient access to their files across devices, as opposed to locally saved files, which are only available on the machine on which they are saved. There are many services designed to facilitate cloud-based file syncing. Some keep files in sync across devices, while others serve as a centralized, cloud-based hard drive. Users trying to select a service should consider the type of functionality they need, as well as factors such as privacy, price, and the operating systems of their computers and their mobile devices, as all of these variables will impact the service they select. This chapter will discuss tools such as Dropbox, SpiderOak, Box, UbuntuOne, SugarSync, SkyDrive, iCloud, ownCloud, and Google Drive, identifying the strengths and weakness of each service, some of which are client oriented and some of which are entirely cloud based.

Key words: Box, Dropbox, file syncing, Google Drive, iCloud, ownCloud, SkyDrive, SpiderOak, SugarSync, UbuntuOne.

Most users are probably used to the traditional file-saving paradigm: files are saved either to a local computer or to some sort of portable device, such as a USB key or portable hard drive. Prior to that, the mode of saving for travel purposes might have involved using a floppy disk of some sort. But historically, if users wanted to take files with them, they had to use some sort of recording medium.

The cloud has revolutionized that process. With the rise in popularity and availability of web-based email, many users took to using email for storing files, emailing work to themselves so it would be available wherever they needed it. On the one hand, this made files easy to transport and easy to access across multiple devices. But, it was not always convenient to find the file that was needed. Or, for that matter, the right version of the right file.

As more and more devices have become available, from smart phones to tablets to netbooks, users find themselves working in more and more locations. The challenge of working with locally saved files is keeping everything in sync. Which version is the latest version? Even using portable recording medium can be problematic, as they (or the data housed on them) can be lost.

For many researchers, the prospect of leaving their main work device becomes comparable to packing for a long trip – they need to consider everything they might need while away from the device and make sure it's available for whatever new device they will be working on. If they forget to copy or email a crucial file, they are out of luck until they are once again in front of their main device.

Luckily, there are now several cloud-based solutions that make storing and accessing files across devices a very convenient and much less stressful prospect.

Dropbox

Dropbox (*www.dropbox.com*) is one of the more popular cloud-based file storage services (Figure 4.1). It's also remarkably easy to use. Users simply download the Dropbox client from the Dropbox site and create a Dropbox account

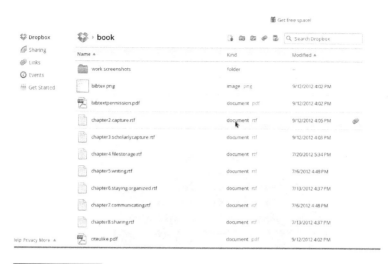

Figure 4.1 Dropbox

(the client is available for Windows, OS X, Linux, and mobile devices). Once the client is installed, there will be a Dropbox folder on the local machine. Any files or folder in that Dropbox folder will be synced against the cloud-based Dropbox servers. Every time a file is updated, the updated file is immediately synced against the Dropbox server (assuming the user has some sort of network connection).

Where Dropbox gets especially useful is in situations where there is more than one device in play. For example a user might install Dropbox on their home laptop. All of their home laptop files in the Dropbox folder are now synced against the Dropbox server. If the they then install Dropbox on a work computer and log into Dropbox using the same credential they used at home, their work Dropbox folder will contain all of the files from their home laptop Dropbox folder. If the user edits any of those files at work, the files on the home laptop will be updated. So while these files exist across multiple machines, Dropbox keeps them in sync.

It gets even more convenient than that, though. Dropbox also has smart phone clients, so a user would have access to their Dropbox files from a phone or tablet. Any files changed on a mobile device would be synced and so the changes would show up on all of the machines on which Dropbox is installed. Dropbox gives users a seamless file-saving experience across devices.

The client automatically syncs files, but Dropbox can be used on machines without the client by using the Dropbox web interface, which allows users to manually upload files to their account as well as download files from their account. Anything uploaded is instantly synced across all devices with the client installed. The web interface is robust, allowing users to upload multiple files at a time and allowing users to download entire folders as compressed files.

Users can also share folders with other Dropbox users. Anyone receiving a shared folder will see that folder in their Dropbox folder. Any files added to that shared folder are instantly seen by anyone invited to share the folder.

Dropbox has a public folder, which allows users to make files publicly available to anyone with the URL for the public folder. Dropbox users can also make folders and files outside of the public folder public accessible. These files and folders can be viewed by anyone, even users without a Dropbox account, and the content displays within the web browser. However, content like this cannot be edited by a non-Dropbox user. Even so, this is a very easy way for researchers to make material available without worrying about changes being made by someone else.

Dropbox gives every user 2 GB of free storage. Users can earn more storage by referring other users, completing certain tasks on their site, and using a .edu email address. There are paid plans with additional storage available to users syncing a lot of data and business plans for multiple users.

Dropbox syncs copies of data but the files are always available on the local machine, so if a user decides to stop using Dropbox, it's simply a matter of uninstalling the client and deleting the account via the web interface. Local files will still be available to the user. Dropbox also lets users manage devices with access to the master account via the web interface, so if they need to deactivate access to a computer or device, they can do so remotely.

Researchers will appreciate a tool like Dropbox because it allows all of their work and research to be available from pretty much anywhere there's a device and network connectivity. For instance, if a researcher was gathering information, they might be collecting articles. Given that so much research is now available electronically, and if they are not using a research management tool (see Chapter 3), they might have a lot of PDFs lying around in a folder on a computer. This is fine as long as the researcher is working on that one computer, but if they are away from that computer, they will not have access to the research saved on that computer. However, using a tool like Dropbox, any articles saved in the Dropbox folder will be available on any machine with the Dropbox client installed, or via the Dropbox web interface. So if the researcher suddenly finds themselves needing an article saved on their home computer, it will be available from anywhere.

This becomes especially useful when considering the role of tablets and mobile devices in this equation. For instance, a user might have a pile of articles they need to read. The articles are PDFs on a home machine and are saved in a Dropbox folder. If they are stuck somewhere, perhaps waiting for an appointment, or a dull meeting, they can access their Dropbox account via their device and call up the articles from the home machine. So even if the user does not have the foresight to take articles along with them on their errands, they still have access to all of their material, even if they are not on a desktop or laptop computer.

The same would hold true for drafts of work, also. Any notes, completed works, or files are available from anywhere via Dropbox, as long as they are saved in the Dropbox folder. Dropbox also saves previous versions of documents, giving you the ability to return to a previously saved version of a document, a very helpful feature if something important is inadvertently overwritten or deleted.

The collaborative aspects of Dropbox are also intriguing. Most collaborative projects involve some degree of emailing unless all parties are in close physical proximity. There's certainly nothing wrong with emailing drafts and articles back and forth, but there can be complications. For instance, what if three people working on a project all make edits on their local machines and then email their version around? Someone must then integrate all of the changes into a single document and email the new version to all collaborators. Dropbox allows for everyone sharing a folder to make changes, with the changes instantly reflected in the folder. Unless collaborators decide to all edit the same file at the same time, the document will continue to evolve without the need to email drafts. Instead, everyone sharing a folder will see a notification that a file has been updated.

The shared folder can also be helpful for sharing research. Rather than emailing electronic articles and books to everyone collaborating on a project, collaborators can instead save their research to a shared folder where everyone will have access to the same material.

If users are working with photos, images, videos, or sound, the shared folder will also work. Dropbox syncs any and all electronic files.

One final advantage of Dropbox from a research perspective is that it serves as a backup for all of a user's work. If a local machine dies or is stolen, all of the work on the machine is gone, unless the user has been diligent about backing up work. Keep in mind that even a weekly backup schedule could mean losing up to a week's worth of work if a device is somehow compromised. Dropbox serves as a backup of all of that work, no matter what happens to the devices on which the work was created or accessed. Dropbox is a safety net for work, which in itself makes it worth considering, even if all of a user's research is conducted and written on one machine.

Dropbox is an excellent product but is not without its challenges. The most important one to consider is the security of the service. Users might be concerned about having all of their files floating in a cloud they do not control. Dropbox maintains the service is secure (Dropbox, n.d.), but in June 2011, there was a temporary security breach that allowed Dropbox users to access any Dropbox account using their own password (McCullagh, 2011). The breach lasted just a few hours but it is something to consider when deciding to move data into Dropbox, or into any cloud-based service.

Another consideration is the impact Dropbox has on the speed of devices. Because Dropbox is constantly monitoring the folders on a machine, it can sometimes slow devices down. Also, when uploading large files, Dropbox can sometimes slow down an entire home network.

Finally, using Dropbox in a collaborative environment is dependent upon having collaborators with Dropbox accounts. If collaborators are invited to share a folder, but they do not want to create Dropbox accounts, they will be able to view but not edit shared materials.

SpiderOak

SpiderOak (*www.spideroak.com*) is another file storage service, comparable to Dropbox (Figure 4.2). Like Dropbox, it works by having users download a client. Unlike Dropbox, which requires all files to be synced to be placed in a Dropbox folder, SpiderOak lets users select whichever folders and files they want synced. This can be a huge advantage to users who are particular about their file hierarchies.

In general, the two services are very similar in how they work and the functionality they offer. The major difference is that while Dropbox is simple, requiring very little decision-making from the user, SpiderOak offers more options and choices, which could make it feel more complicated to certain kinds of users.

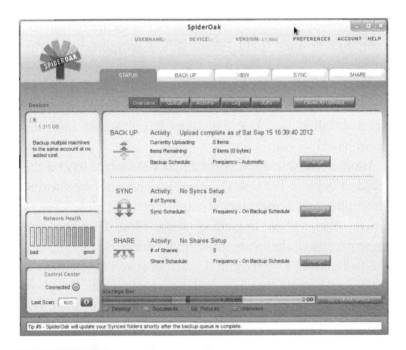

Figure 4.2 SpiderOak

For instance, files can be shared in Dropbox by right clicking on a folder and clicking the option that says *Share This Folder*. In SpiderOak, sharing folders is done through the client, with users creating a ShareID and a RoomKey and then sharing the information with collaborators. The SpiderOak client has a few tabs, with lots of options in each, while Dropbox provides an information area that rarely needs to be used.

SpiderOak's syncing ability is also more nuanced than Dropbox's, with users able to select different folders to sync on each machine, meaning a user might keep the article drafts on one machine synced but not the photos, while another device might have its photos synced, but not the article drafts. Given that SpiderOak has a 2 GB file size limit on its free tier, just like Dropbox, users can conserve space by only syncing the files they need from each individual machine, rather than syncing everything.

SpiderOak, like Dropbox, has a web interface, although the Dropbox web interface is much smoother and easier to use. Also, users cannot upload documents into SpiderOak via the web interface. Also like Dropbox, SpiderOak has clients for PCs, Macs, and Linux, as well as Android and iOS devices.

The research applications for SpiderOak are comparable with Dropbox. However, the more detailed SpiderOak client might appeal to users who want to take a more active role in what data is synced and backed up, as well as how often that happens.

SpiderOak's sharing mechanism is not as simple as Dropbox's right-click functionality. However, SpiderOak does allow users to share content via secure links and provides optional password protection. The advantage over Dropbox's sharing is that the person with whom the content is being shared does not need a SpiderOak account to see it.

Dropbox allows users to share content in a public folder, but, in theory, anyone with the URL for that folder would have access to all of the content within it. Depending upon the content, this could be an uncomfortable privacy situation. However, the SpiderOak share is one-way, meaning one person is sharing content with another person, but the person being shared with cannot upload content into the shared folder. This does not provide the same collaborative possibilities with Dropbox sharing, which might be an issue for some researchers.

Although the collaboration functionality within SpiderOak is not as intuitive as it is within Dropbox, a user committed to using SpiderOak could certainly figure out a flow for sharing material. As mentioned previously, SpiderOak allows the user to customize more backup and syncing aspects than Dropbox. The cost for that customization is in the interface, which can be a bit complex to navigate, requiring the user to make certain choices in terms of which folders and files are backed up, as well as how often that occurs.

SpiderOak's mobile client gives users the potential to access their content from anywhere, which can be convenient in any number of situations. It also has an institutional version designed specifically for educational institutions. Interested users might see if their local institution has a subscription.

Google Drive

Google Drive (*drive.google.com*) is Google's entry into the cloud-based file storage market (Figure 4.3), a market it surprisingly did not enter until April 2012. Like many of the

Figure 4.3 Google Drive

other tools discussed in this chapter, Google Drive uses a client to facilitate file storage and transfer, but also has a robust and effective web interface.

The Google Drive concept is similar to some of the other services discussed within this chapter. Users download the client and the client creates a folder. Files placed in the folder are synced into Google Drive. Where Google Drive differs is in its integration with Google's web-based word processor (see Chapter 5). Google Drive also places links to Google Docs documents in the local Google Drive folder. This gives users another access point into a Google Doc file. It is important to note that these files are not the actual files, but rather shortcut links into Google Docs. If a user does not have connectivity, they will not have access to the content within the files (while the Chrome browser supports offline Google Docs editing, not everyone uses Chrome as their default browser and Google Drive uses the default browser to open Google Docs links). Users can also opt not to sync Google Docs files in their local Google Drive folder.

Users can save word-processed files into their Google Drive. The files, whatever their format, will show up within the web-based Google Drive interface, which is also the Google Docs interface (Google merged the two products into a single concept). For supported file types, users will be able to view the file within the Google Docs interface, but they will not be able to edit it unless the file is exported from the Google Drive web interface into Google Docs. This is where Google Drive can get confusing. Some files will be editable but some files will not, depending on how the file was originally created. Files not created with Google Docs but synced with Google Drive will need to be exported into Google Drive for online editing. This would not be much of an issue for users who do not intend to edit any documents online.

The sharing of Google Drive files must be managed through the Google Drive web interface and is the same process as seen in Google Docs document sharing, with all of the strengths and weaknesses of that process. Items that have been shared with a user via Google Drive or Google Docs do not automatically appear in the local Google Drive folder. Users must manually add those files created by someone else to their local Google Drive folder.

Google Drive offers 5 GB of free storage, with an option to buy more storage for a monthly fee. The Google Drive client is available for OS X and Windows, but not Linux. There is also an Android and iOS client.

Box

Box (*www.box.net*) is another file-sharing option (Figure 4.4). Initially there was no client, with Box being entirely web-based (although it did have mobile clients). Users

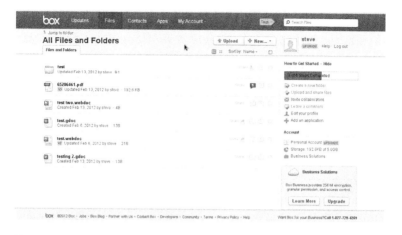

Figure 4.4 Box

manually uploaded files to Box and could either access them when needed or share the files with other users. With the client now available, users can have files sync automatically, without having to manually upload content, and can control the access levels of files, with more controls available to users who upgrade to a paid account. Users can also invite collaborators into folders, giving the collaborator the right to add and edit content within the shared folder, or simply access to view the content. The free, basic account starts users off with 5 GB of space.

Box also has what it calls Apps. These are programs that integrate with other sites and programs. For instance, Box has a Microsoft Office app that allows users to save files directly to their Box account via Office. It also allows users to open files stored in Box via Office. The Office app is free, but as of this writing is only available for PC users. It is worth noting that there are other ways to obtain similar functionality. For instance, LibreOffice has a built-in option that allows users to export documents into either Google

Drive or Zoho (see Chapter 5). Google Cloud Connect (available via *tools.google.com/dlpage/cloudconnect*) provides similar integration between Microsoft Office and Google Docs, but is only available for PC users.

Box is more than just file storage, though. It also has a content creation element. Users can create documents and bookmarks from within the Box web interface. It also allows users to create Google Docs documents via the Box web interface.

The file editing capabilities within Box are interesting. Users collaborating on a paper could easily make changes and share ideas without having to open a word processor. Box also allows users to preview documents within the web interface, which saves downloading if they just need to quickly access a document from a computer on which they do not usually work.

Users working with a lot of files, or a few huge files (Box can accommodate files up to 100 MB), might be intrigued by the ability of Box to accommodate their space needs on a free tier.

Box's sharing capabilities are simple to use and to understand. Users can choose to share files or folders, with the folders and files either publicly available or limited to collaborators (who must have Box accounts to access the material). Content can be viewable or editable. Once a user has determined who they want to be able to access content within their Box account and what the user should be able to do with the content, it's simple to configure settings for the folder or file. It's also simple to change settings.

Box allows users to comment on content, with the comments displaying within the Box web interface, providing immediate feedback without having to open a file. It also has highly configurable notifications, so users can track when content is added or changed. Like Dropbox and

SpiderOak, Box has mobile clients, giving users access to their files from just about anywhere.

Box is cloud-based file access at its simplest and, for some users, Box is too simple. While Box does offer the interesting ability to edit files within its web interface, that ability also exists within other web tools (see Chapter 5). The Box client is available for Windows and OS X.

Ubuntu One

Ubuntu One (*one.ubuntu.com*) is an unusual tool in that it originated as a file-syncing service for the Ubuntu operating system, a version of Linux (Figure 4.5). It's much like Dropbox or SpiderOak, with users downloading a client that then syncs their data against a web server. What's

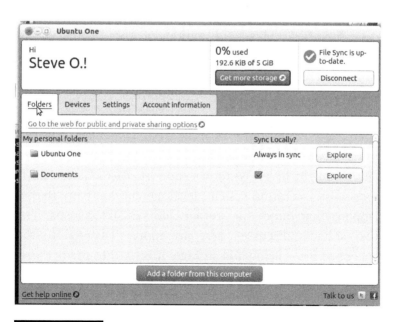

Figure 4.5 Ubuntu One

interesting about Ubuntu One is that the service has branched away from the Ubuntu operating system. There is now a client for Windows, OS X, and mobile clients for Android and iOS. That dramatically opens up the potential audience for Ubuntu One.

Ubuntu One is comparable to the other services discussed here. Users choose which folders to sync, and they can share folders with other users, although, like Dropbox, non-public folders require a login to be shared. Users can also make files public if they wish to share something with a broader audience. Users might be interested in Ubuntu One because of the 5 GB of storage it provides on its free tier, with additional storage available for sale.

Ubuntu One gives users persistent access to their files and allows users to share files and folders. Ubuntu One folders can be shared with a user and the user can be given the right to make changes to a folder, meaning they can upload and change files. They can also prevent shared folders from being modified. This is a hybrid of the Dropbox and SpiderOak sharing models. Ubuntu One limits which folders can be synced, so not every folder on your computer might be syncable, as is the case with Dropbox.

Ubuntu One was designed for the Ubuntu operating system. While the Windows and OS X clients work now, it's hard to say how committed Canonical, the company behind Ubuntu, might be to Windows support. Also, Canonical is more of an operating system development company than a company that builds file storage and syncing systems. The other services discussed here are more dedicated to the concept of file syncing and storage. It is hard to predict how long any web-based service might last, but the fact that Ubuntu One is not Canonical's main project is a valid matter of concern for some users.

Ubuntu One cannot be used on most other Linux distributions.

SugarSync

SugarSync (*www.sugarsync.com*) is comparable to Dropbox, SpiderOak, and Ubuntu One in that it's a downloadable client that allows the user to select syncable folders (Figure 4.6). SugarSync allows users to select which folders are synced and/or backed up. SugarSync, which starts users with 5 GB of space, is more client-oriented than any of the other services discussed. Users choose which folders are synced, but synced folders and files are only available through the SugarSync client. So whereas Dropbox and SpiderOak provide a unified experience where users access files via folders on their local computer, in SugarSync, synced files from another computer must be accessed through the client. For files users want to share across computers, there is a special file folder called Magic Briefcase, which syncs all files within the folder across computers and devices where SugarSync is installed.

Like the other tools discussed, SugarSync has a web interface. Folders can be shared with users and files can be made public. SugarSync has the standard sharing tools seen

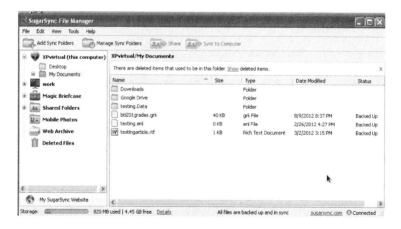

Figure 4.6 SugarSync

in the other file managers discussed here. Users wishing to access a shared folder will need to create a SugarSync account. Folders can be shared and users can then sync a shared folder to their local computer, creating a Dropbox-like shared folder, where updates are propagated across machines and devices. This can be very helpful for collaborative research. But even researchers working alone will appreciate the flexibility of choosing which folders to back up and which to sync, giving users a custom file overview from which to work.

SugarSync is also great at making work public and downloadable. Every file can be made public and given a URL that can be shared. There's no limit on the size of any file being shared, so users can easily share huge files with a broad audience.

SugarSync has a variety of mobile clients, including iOS, Android, BlackBerry, Windows Mobile and Symbian. The SugarSync client is only available for PC and Mac, leaving Linux users out in the cold. SugarSync, like SpiderOak, requires some user configuration. Users must choose which folders they want backed up and which ones they want synced and determining file needs could prove complicated for some users.

SkyDrive

SkyDrive (*skydrive.live.com*) is Microsoft's cloud-based file storage service (Figure 4.7). Users start with a generous 7 GB of storage for their documents. Like other tools discussed, there is a client, but it is only available for Windows and OS X. There is also a mobile client for Android, iOS and for Windows phones.

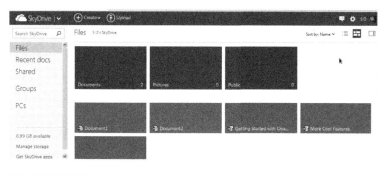

Figure 4.7 SkyDrive

Like Box, SkyDrive allows users to create and edit documents within the browser. Users can share documents and folders, requiring a SkyDrive login, if wanted. Users can also indicate whether a folder or file is editable. SkyDrive's collaborative capabilities are nuanced, which should allow most users to share their work in a manner that makes sense to them.

SkyDrive, like Box and Google Drive, has built-in document creation and editing capabilities. Users can create Word, Excel, and PowerPoint documents within the browser, saving them to their SkyDrive. Uploaded documents can then be viewed and edited within the SkyDrive, without having to download the files. Because so much academic writing seems to take place within Microsoft Office, SkyDrive's tight integration with Office is especially convenient.

SkyDrive is very much a competitor to Google Drive. In fact, the tool has evolved to become easier to use and should look very familiar to those already familiar with Google Drive. SkyDrive might not have the cache of Google Drive, coming as it does from Microsoft, a company that, up until recently, has been reluctant to embrace the cloud, but it's a solid tool created by an established company. Users trying to avoid Google might be surprised to see how well Microsoft can accommodate them.

ownCloud

ownCloud (*www.owncloud.com*) is software that can be installed on a web server (Figure 4.8), allowing users to have their own cloud-based file management solution, hosted on a server the user controls (although ownCloud does link users to hosted solutions, where the server is owned and maintained by a third party). ownCloud is a space for users to upload, share, and even edit files. It is open source software, meaning the code is collaboratively developed and maintained.

ownCloud is not as robust as most of the tools described in this chapter. It's basically a web space where users can upload files. The web interface allows users to manually upload and download files, and share them with certain groups. For users just looking for a secure online place to park their work, this could represent a good solution, especially for those concerned about privacy and the long-term viability of some of the companies creating these file management services.

Users must install and maintain ownCloud themselves, unless they use a hosted solution or pay for a subscription of some kind. That means if anything goes wrong with the software, the user might need to troubleshoot the problem themselves. Also, because the software is open source, there is no guarantee the developers will continue to work on the project.

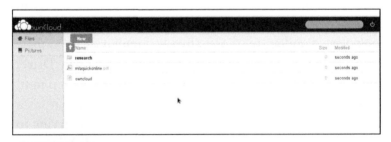

Figure 4.8   ownCloud

ownCloud does not have a lot of the nuanced functionality seen in some of the tools discussed here. It is very basic and requires the manual uploading and downloading of files, although, because the project is open source, there is always the chance someone might develop a more robust client.

iCloud

Apple's iCloud service is an example of a service designed to keep data in sync across devices. Of course, given that Apple is a hardware vendor, the service privileges Apple hardware, but for certain users, it's a perfectly acceptable solution.

iCloud allows users to sync their data across devices, so that something available on a laptop is also available on an iOS device. The idea is that documents can be available anywhere iCloud is installed. While iCloud is optimized for Apple hardware, there is a PC client that allows PC users to sync their data, making it available on an iOS device such as an iPod or iPad, or available via iCloud's web interface.

The basic iCloud starts users off with 5 GB of free space. Like many of the tools discussed so far, iCloud's strength is its ability to give users persistent access to their files across computers and devices. iCloud can also sync content purchased from iTunes, which might include books. If a user's research involves books purchased from iTunes, this persistent access could be helpful.

The major challenge of using iCloud arises if a user is not heavily invested in Apple hardware. iCloud only works on iOS mobile devices, so Android users looking to use their mobile devices to access material synced on their computers will find themselves very frustrated. iCloud is optimized for the iWork office suite. While Office documents should be fine, there might be formatting issues working between Office and iWork documents.

If a user becomes heavily invested in iCloud, they might find it difficult to leave Apple hardware. For instance, while a current iPhone user might love iCloud, that user now must maintain access to an iOS device or face losing mobile access to their documents.

Conclusion

So which tool should a user select? The user needs to consider how they'll be working. For instance, if they want files to be automatically synced to the cloud, they might want to rule out something like Box, which lacks a desktop client. If the user is on a Linux computer, they should probably rule out SugarSync, which does not have a Linux client at the moment.

In general, though, Dropbox seems to be very popular with lots of users around the Internet, because of its ease of use. However, for power users, something more configureable, such as SpiderOak or SugarSync, might be better starting points. Users already immersed in the Google system might consider Google Drive as the path of least resistance, although it is not as fully featured as many of the tools discussed in this chapter.

SkyDrive and Google Drive, and to a lesser extent, Box, are interesting in that they are blurring the line between file creation and file storage. These tools help users not only to save and retrieve files, but also provide a cloud-based way for users to meaningfully work with the files, too.

Users will also want to investigate the security of a potential tool, to see if it matches their expectations.

Depending upon the size of files that need to be synced, service pricing will also be an issue, although all of the tools discussed here have free service tiers that should provide more than enough storage for users to get a sense of if a particular service is a good match.

In terms of free storage, as more services enter the field, more free storage will be in play, as services try to entice new users. However, as the field shrinks, which might be expected given the volume of services entering the market every few months, those that survive might see less reason to offer a large amount of free storage to users who do not have many options. It would probably be as well not to get to accustomed to too much free storage over the long term.

Whichever tool users select, they will be amazed at the convenience of having access to all of their files from any computer or device. They will no longer need to worry about misplaced thumb drives or forgetting to email themselves the one file they need to finish their work. And for users working collaboratively, they'll see the potential time savings available from having automatically shared files that everyone working on the project can access.

5

Writing in the cloud

Abstract: The traditional model for word processing has been client-based, with users using a locally installed program, usually Microsoft Word, to compose and edit documents. Cloud-based word processors allow users to edit and compose from any desktop computer with a web browser, regardless of what, if any, word processing clients are locally installed. Cloud-based word processors also tend to make collaboration easier, as many have built-in tools to facilitate collaboration across both time and space. For users unable or uninterested in cloud-based word processors, text files and Rich Text Format documents represent another option in collaborating on content without focusing upon document formatting. This chapter discusses cloud-based word processors such as Google Drive, Zoho Writer and the Microsoft Word Web App, but also discusses nontraditional composition tools, such as the PBworks wiki, and two web-based text editors, Yahoo! Notepad and SimpleNote.

Key words: Google Docs, Google Drive, Rich Text Format, Simplenote, Word, word processing, Zoho.

Writing is a personal act and also a solitary one. Ask ten different academics how and where they do their writing and ten different responses might be heard. One might write on a desktop computer in their on-campus office; another might use a laptop in a coffee shop. But if there's variety in the places where academics write, there is probably less variation in their choice of composition tool: many of them write with Microsoft Word.

There are reasons for this. Microsoft Word's proprietary document format is often the preferred way for users to exchange documents. Word is also still popular in enterprise settings, including universities. As a Gartner report stated quite explicitly, "Microsoft Office cannot be eliminated" (Silver, 2011). Because it cannot be eliminated, it continues to be used.

Cloud-based word processing tools are attractive options to many users, though. For one thing, they are usually free, where Microsoft Office might have some charges associated with it, depending upon the Office licensing at the user's institution. There are free-of-cost word processors such as LibreOffice and Apache OpenOffice, but even if cost is taken off of the table, client-based word processors, such as Word, LibreOffice, or Apache OpenOffice, have their disadvantages. For example, clients usually need to be installed. Depending upon the number of work places a user has, installation could represent a significant time investment.

Client-based tools also often require the syncing of documents, although as shown in Chapter 4, and as will be discussed in this chapter, many word processors are embracing the cloud in their approach to file management.

The appeal of cloud-based word processors is their simplicity. Users just go to a browser and begin typing. It can be done from just about any browser on any operating system. All you need, usually, is an Internet connection of some kind.

Cloud-based word processors can often make collaboration easier. As seen in Chapter 4, there are many ways for users to easily share files with each other, but cloud-based word processors can be just as simple, without requiring the use of a file-syncing service. Many cloud-based word processors will also automatically track the history of a document, so users can see changes to the document over time. This kind of functionality is available in Microsoft Word, but needs to be activated by the user.

Cloud-based word processors usually have the ability to interact with Word in some way, in terms of both importing and exporting Word documents. This means that for situations that require a Word document, either to start or to complete a project, cloud-based word processors are still a viable option.

Google Drive

Google Drive (*drive.google.com/*), previously known as Google Docs, is probably one of the more popular cloud-based word processors (Figure 5.1). A free product from Google, it allows users to generate a word-processed document in their web browser. Google Drive also allows users to create spreadsheets, presentations (à la Microsoft PowerPoint), forms, and drawings.

Users can also upload existing documents and convert them into Google documents. Google Drive supports Microsoft Word documents (**.doc** and **.docx**), html files, plain text documents (**.txt**) and Rich Text Format documents (**.rtf**). It does not support native older Apache OpenOffice documents (**.sxw**) or Open Document Format documents (**.odt**), which are commonly used in Apache OpenOffice/ LibreOffice documents.

The Google Drive interface should look familiar to Word users when they are writing or editing documents. No cloud-based word processor will have all the functionality of a client-based one, but users will be able to accomplish basic

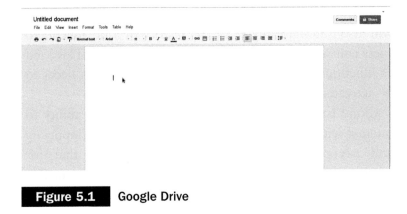

Figure 5.1   Google Drive

word processing functions, such as indenting text, building simple tables, changing fonts, and applying bold or italics to text.

Google Drive is also an intriguing tool for collaboration. Documents are private by default, but users can choose to share a document with specific users (or groups), who will need a Google credential to access the document. Users can also choose to make a document publicly viewable. Where it gets interesting is if two people are editing a document at the same time. Google Drive will show the edits as they are being made by the collaborators, with an indication of who is making the changes. The experience is much like sitting with another user in front of a single word processor and writing a document together, except that with Google Drive, the experience might be occurring across space.

Google Drive also has a built-in chat room that appears when more than one user is viewing a document, which allows a side conversation to take place outside the document itself. Google Drive also supports comments within the document, with users notified when a comment has been made.

The Google+ social networking service also has a Google Drive feature. Google+ allows users to chat via video camera using a Google+ feature called Hangouts. Google Drive is integrated with Hangouts so that a Google document can be open within the Hangout area for users to discuss and edit. This feature makes Google Drive remarkably like users sitting in front of a word processor, composing a single document together. All of these tools facilitate the face-to-virtual-face development of a document by consensus in an easy way.

Another potential benefit involves Google Apps, which offers Google services, including Google Drive, with integration for users on the same domain. The specific domain aspect is helpful, because, in theory, all users at an institution should have email addresses from the same domain. Google Apps allows users to restrict document access at the domain level, so only users with an institutional email address can share or edit a document. A researcher could make a document available to everyone with an institutional email address, meaning anyone from the institution could access and/or edit a document, but the document would be inaccessible to users from outside the institution. The Google Apps implementation of Google Drive allows users to share documents with other users outside the domain, but an informational warning is displayed whenever someone tries this. This functionality is only available to users whose institutions use Google Apps. Google Apps is no longer free for individuals.

Depending upon the implementation, users might need to associate an institutional email address with a Google account. In general, users who wish to implement something like this will need to consult their local IT department. But much of this functionality is also quite achievable with the standard Google Drive. Details on Google Apps for Education can be found at *www.google.com/apps/intl/en/edu/*. Details on the service for businesses (or interested individuals) can be found at *www.google.com/intx/en/ enterprise/apps/business/*.

Once documents are saved, they appear on a list of the user's Google files. They can be organized into folders and/ or sorted, much like in a desktop file manager.

There is one final consideration about Google Drive versus a desktop word processor. Online, there are many conversations around the idea of the distraction-free writing environment, a concept brought into the mainstream by Virginia Heffernan (2008). Distraction-free writing environments are word processors with simple interfaces, allowing the user to focus on writing and not on formatting or typesetting. These types of tools also tend to take up the entire computer screen, so the user cannot see what is going on in the background of their computer. Those interested can create a similar type of interface with Google Drive, by choosing its full screen view, which is under the View menu. This view hides all of Google Drive's controls, such as font name and size, and indentation. Users can also choose to hide the ruler along the top of Google Drive by using the View menu, which leaves a simple interface. It can be simplified further by putting the browser into full-screen mode (that option is found under the browser's View menu; the F11 key also works for most browsers), so that the browser takes up the entire screen, with nothing visible but the document at hand. Google Drive suddenly provides a quick and easy distraction-free writing environment that does not require purchasing or installing any software.

Depending upon a user's workflow and browser-choice, printing from Google Drive might be considered inconvenient. It isn't possible to print directly from a non-Chrome browser. Instead, on browsers such as Internet Explorer and Firefox, users must download their documents as PDFs and then print the PDFs. Google Drive makes the issue slightly less confusing by having the print dialogue trigger a PDF download, but it still makes printing a two-step process. Chrome browser users have some additional Google Drive functionality, besides printing, for example they can configure Google Drive to provide offline document access for when there is no Internet connection. That option is within the Google Drive settings area.

Google Drive is available as an Android and iOS app and is usable as a web-based application on many smart phones and tablets, including iOS and Android. LibreOffice Writer, a client-based word processor, also has a built-in option to export documents directly into Google Drive, an interesting mix of cloud and client.

No discussion of a Google service is complete without a discussion of the privacy implications. The early 2012 changes to Google's privacy policy allows Google to share user information across Google services, presumably creating a fairly impressive user profile. For instance, the new privacy policy allows Google to show ads to users based on what they might be writing about in a Google document, which is dismaying for many users (Garside, 2012). There is no way to opt out of the Google policy. Users who do not wish to have their data connected by Google must instead find another service.

Microsoft Word Web App

If Google Drive is the conceptual version of the cloud-based Word, Word Web App (skydrive.live.com) is the literal cloud-based version of it (Figure 5.2). As discussed in Chapter 4, Word Web App allows users to create Word (as well as PowerPoint, Excel, and OneNote) documents in their browser. It provides some direct integration with Word,

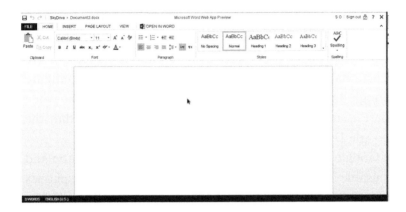

Figure 5.2   Microsoft Word Web App

allowing users to open the cloud-based version of documents in their local version of Word.

Like Google Drive, Word Web App allows users to perform basic editing tasks. Unlike Google Apps, Word Web App does not offer much in the way of collaboration tools. Word Web App will generate links with certain privileges, such as view only, or view and edit, but the privileges are associated with the link and not with specific users, so anyone with the link (and an Outlook account) would have the same level of access. Word Web App also does not offer any chat and has very limited simultaneous editing capabilities, so that it is often more like one person working at a time after a browser refresh. However, these are not major issues for users who do not intend to collaborate in real time on their writing projects.

A major advantage to Word Web App its ability to integrate with Word so well. Because the Word .doc and .docx formats are proprietary, Microsoft is in the best position to translate and create documents around the format. Non-Microsoft tools, such as Google Drive, often lose formatting in the move from the tool into Microsoft Word. With Word Web App, presumably less should be lost in translation.

Microsoft has a mobile client for Windows mobile, Android, and iOS that allows users to access but not edit their Word Web App files. There is also a mobile site that allows smart phone and tablet users to view but not edit their documents.

Word Web App and its mobile clients are free.

Zoho Writer

Zoho is a collection of web-based applications that includes services such as email, calendars, wikis, and, unsurprisingly given the subject of this chapter, word processors (Figure 5.3). Zoho Writer (*writer.zoho.com/*) is similar to Google Drive and Word Web App in that it allows users to type and manipulate text using their web browser. Users can import a variety of formats, including Open Document Formatting (.odt) and Apache OpenOffice (.sxw), and WordPerfect (**.wpd**) native files. Zoho Writer also lets users import Google

Figure 5.3   Zoho Writer

documents directly from Google Drive. Like Google Drive, Zoho Writer has fairly robust sharing capabilities, allowing users to share with groups and individuals.

Zoho Writer's main advantage is that it is not Google. For users uncomfortable with Google's privacy policy, Zoho represents a viable alternative, although users probably want to consult Zoho's privacy policy to make sure it conforms to their expectations: *www.zoho.com/privacy.html*.

Like Google and Word Web App, Zoho Writer has a mobile site, but unlike Google Drive's mobile site, users cannot edit Zoho Writer documents within the mobile browser. LibreOffice Writer also has an option for users to export documents directly into Zoho Writer.

Zoho is free for personal use.

PBworks

PBworks (*pbworks.com*) is a wiki, meaning, in theory, it's designed to be a web page that anyone can edit (Figure 5.4). But PBworks is more productivity software than pure wiki and allows users to maintain private spaces that only the

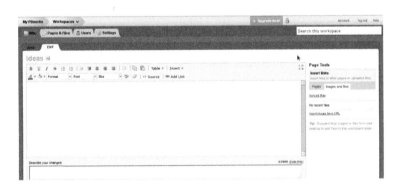

Figure 5.4   PBworks

user or their collaborators can access. This makes PBworks an interesting composition tool, in that it's not entirely designed for composition and is instead designed for sharing information. However, it still works quite well for creating content, if not for word-processing.

Wikis, in their purest form, are websites that anyone, or only certain users, can edit from within their browser. That means the default mode for a wiki is view, with the assumption that most wiki users are viewing the information on the wiki, rather than creating or editing it. Should a user decide to make a change to a wiki, and assuming they have permission, they'll click an edit link and will then have the ability to make changes to the page. This workflow differs from how one uses a modern word processor, where users can edit or add content without having to toggle into an edit mode. This extra step separates PBworks from most word processors, either cloud- or client-based.

PBworks' edit mode behaves more like a traditional word processor, allowing users to type text and perform basic formatting. However, one important and significant difference lies in how PBworks allows users to export their work. Because it is not a traditional word processor, PBworks does not have a Word/RTF export function. Instead, users must either export their work as a PDF of their wiki page, or they must copy and paste their PBworks document into a word processor, and then reformat the document.

Despite the fact that PBworks is not intended for use as a word processor and despite the hurdle that using it as such requires a multi-step process, it is still an intriguing option for some users. For instance, it is a very easy space for collaboration, allowing users to be notified of changes made to the wiki, either via email or **RSS**. It also allows users to view the history of a document, seeing changes that were made, and even comparing page versions against each other.

Users also have the option of reverting to an older version of a document in case some recent changes turn out to be a poor idea (Google Drive has a similar functionality that allows users to see the revision history of a document and revert to a previous version).

One of PBworks' most useful collaborative features is its ability to allow users to create accounts for other users. Most of the collaborative tools discussed within this chapter, and within this book, allow collaboration, but require users to create accounts with the service to allow collaboration. For certain users, this presents a barrier, as it requires the potential collaborator to create yet another account, a process which some users resist. But PBworks users can create accounts for users of their wiki, so instead of depending upon a collaborator to create an account (and regularly remember password and login information), a user can create an account for a collaborator and send them the login and password. No email account or personal information is needed; the wiki owner just needs to create a login and password, or ask PBworks to come up with one. This simple step makes it that much easier to get a collaborator into a wiki. The trick to implementing this feature is to declare a wiki is for educational purposes and not for individuals. The user is presented with this option when first creating a wiki. The account creation option, called *Classroom Accounts* and found under *Settings*, is only available in education wikis.

PBworks is free for non-commercial use. Users on the free tier can create a number of workspaces, which is what PBworks calls its wikis. The wikis can accommodate a number of pages. Users can also upload files to their wikis, so it accommodates and facilitates a number of working styles. Using PBworks is not as straightforward as some of the other tools discussed in this chapter, but for users looking for a simple writing environment that allows easy collaboration, it presents an interesting option. In the end, many users might find it more useful for brainstorming and organizing, rather than preparing work for publication, but that does not make it any less valuable a tool.

Simplenote

Simplenote (*simplenoteapp.com/*) is a web-based text editor (Figure 5.5). If a user reads through productivity sites, they will discover a certain affinity for text files (which have a.txt file extension), the simple files created with a program such as Windows Notepad or OS X TextEdit. Text files don't allow for any formatting, and instead are simple files of text, perhaps modified with some spaces. Because text files are so simple, they are easy to open across operating systems, with no formatting lost between machines because there is no formatting to lose. Any kind of computing device from within the past few decades should be able to open a text file without much difficulty. Text files are smaller than word-processed files, so they tend to not take up too much

Figure 5.5   Simplenote

space, wherever they are. The lack of formatting in text files also makes them a distraction-free writing environment, although obviously that depends more upon the text editor being used than the format itself. Simplenote, as the name implies, builds on the simplicity of text files.

Within the Simplenote interface, all users can do is type text. There is no other formatting available, although it does support the use of Markdown syntax (Markdown is a popular text-to-HTML conversion tool [Gruber, 2004]). Users just type text into the Simplenote web interface. Users cannot bold, italicize or indent text, although they can create paragraphs. Users can save multiple files within Simplenote, and can share files and publish them on the web. They have access to their notes, which can actually be full work drafts, if they are so inclined, from anywhere they have access to a web browser. Simplenote also tracks revisions, although changes aren't as easy to view as within Google Drive or PBworks. Files can be imported, depending upon the format of the note. Plain text notes are obviously supported.

If this was all Simplenote did, it would be an interesting option for users who want a very simple web interface in which to input text. But where it excels is in its ability to interact with other cloud-based services, as well as clients. These clients, available for Windows, OS X, Linux, Android, and iOS, allow users quick and easy access to their Simplenote files – they can easily move between devices and maintain access to their work. Because users are working with simple plain text files, editing and composing on mobile devices is a simple, viable enterprise. A list of tools and clients can be found at *simplenoteapp.com/downloads/*.

There are also Simplenote extensions designed to integrate with web browsers, allowing users to create and edit files without having to navigate to the Simplenote site.

Like PBworks, Simplenote is not a word processor, so users will need to eventually move their work out of Simplenote for proper formatting, which represents an additional step when compared to some of the other cloud-based word processors discussed here. This could represent a learning curve for anyone accustomed to working with word processors and more formatted documents. But for those already in the habit of working with text files, Simplenote represents the ability to make any device into a text editor, with convenient access to all of their files.

Yahoo! Notepad

Another interesting cloud-based text editor is Yahoo! Notepad (*notepad.yahoo.com/*) (Figure 5.6). Yahoo! Notepad is brilliant in its simplicity. Upon signing in, users have just two options: to add a note or to add a folder. Folders are used to organize notes, with a folder hierarchy displaying on the left side of the screen, allowing navigation to previously saved notes. New notes can be given titles and assigned folders, but that is the extent of the functionality;

Figure 5.6   Yahoo! Notepad

there is no ability to share and no integration with any other services. There are also no formatting options: users type into a web-based text box and save their work when they are done. They can either then print the note or copy and paste the text into a more fully-featured tool when they are ready to format their work.

Users probably would not want to spend extended periods of time working in Yahoo! Notepad, but for anyone looking for a quick and easily accessible place to jot down notes or ideas, without having to deal with a lot of options, Yahoo! Notepad represents an intriguing option that is usually well outside of the cloud-based word processing conversation.

Sharing files

This chapter has discussed many of the cloud-based options for users to write, but for many users and for various reasons, sometimes the cloud is not a realistic option for writing. This probably is not an issue for users who are working alone, but for those who are collaborating on a project, the absence of a cloud-based word processor could make work more challenging. Chapter 4 discusses some potential solutions that focus on cloud-based file management as opposed to cloud-based word processing. The challenge of collaborating via cloud-based file management is when users are writing in different word processors, or on different operating systems. Formatting can be lost and sometimes files cannot even be opened (anyone unfamiliar with this phenomenon has probably never asked students to submit work electronically). To a certain extent, this can be hard to avoid when dealing with proprietary file formats. However, there are certain steps users can take to minimize format incompatibilities.

The first step would be to standardize the word processor being used. If one user is using Word and the other is using WordPerfect, there are probably going to be some compatibility issues. Collaborators agreeing on a word processing tool will go a long way toward improving compatibility. Even when files are saved in the same format, like a WordPerfect user saving files as a Word .doc file, there might still be some issues with incompatible formatting that are exacerbated as the file moves between programs. Sometimes there will even be an issue between the same program used on two different operating systems or two different versions of the same word processor.

If agreeing upon a word processor is not an issue or does not solve compatibility issues, another option is the underrated RTF file format. RTF files preserve some formatting between word processors and operating systems and while it's not a universal format that works seamlessly between programs, for simply-formatted documents, it's an excellent option. The option to save a file as an RTF is found under the *save as* dialogue of most word processors. Once within the dialogue, users can choose a file type of RTF.

Of course, text files are another option, the major drawback being text files preserve no formatting at all. However, despite that limitation, their flexibility does make them an intriguing option.

Users collaborating on a text file might want to consider one of the file-syncing services discussed in Chapter 4 as a centralized location for the text file. This would allow all users access to the file, without having to email copies around to collaborators.

Because of the simplicity of text files, each user would then be free to use the text editor of their choice, without having to achieve any kind of consensus. Windows users could use something like Notepad++ (*notepad-plus-plus.org/*), a free and open source text editor that includes features such as a spellchecker. OS X users could use something like Notational Velocity (*notational.net/*), which is also free and open source, but offers direct integration with Simplenote. Linux users might use something like gedit, the default text editor on many distributions. There is also a gedit client for Windows.

The choice of a text editor is a personal one, so the flexibility to choose one based purely on personal preference, without having to get others to agree, is quite valuable. Also, as mentioned above, most mobile devices can easily edit text files, whereas users cannot assume a device can edit Word, or even RTF files.

A final advantage to collaborating on a single text file is more a compositional one than a technical one. By focusing on text and not the display of the text, collaborators, or even someone working alone, might find themselves more focused on content, and less so on the presentation of the content. This is the logic behind the distraction-free writing environment concept.

Conclusion

The challenge of cloud-based word processing is not tools or options so much as file formats. Right now, Microsoft Word is the de facto document format standard, but because it's a proprietary format, it is not a standard to which all tools can conform. For lightly formatted documents, this is probably not a huge issue, as most of the word processors discussed here can probably export as a .doc/.docx file that will render correctly enough when moving from a cloud-based tool into Word proper, with the Microsoft Word Web App obviously having a huge advantage over the other tools. But more formatted documents, with features like tables and images, might prove more challenging to translate from the cloud to Word, or Word to the cloud.

If a user is interested in composing in something other than Word, whether for political, aesthetic, economic, or collaborative reasons, they should consider the complexity of the document that will be built. A fairly standard article, without anything potentially challenging to translate, such as formulas, will probably render in a straightforward manner. A fairly rigorous template, which some publishers request their authors to use for composing, might not fare as well. The challenge of file formats actually makes the case for some of the cloud-based tools discussed here that are unable to export into a word-processing format. If a user winds up needing to reformat a document, why not just format at the end? Tools such as Simplenote and PBworks do not work with Word, so, if a user is looking to write in a cloud-based environment, they might consider writing in one of those tools, copying and pasting the text into Microsoft Word, and then formatting the entire document before submission.

In fact, users might be impressed by the sparse interface of a tool such as Simplenote or Yahoo! Notepad, which are really nothing more than empty text boxes in a browser. Without font, spacing, and indentation options, users really have no choice but to focus on their words. Some users might find the lack of options very limiting but others might find it liberating. For those who find it a pleasant experience, they might be tempted to take advantage of the simple text editors available in just about every operating system, including mobile ones such as Android and iOS.

A final consideration is a researcher's collaborators and any cloud-based tools they might already be invested in. If two users are using two separate tools, collaboration will be more challenging than if the users are both invested in the same tool. In terms of collaboration, Google Drive is tough to beat, acting as a well-featured word processor, but also as a powerful collaboration tool that supports synchronous and asynchronous revisions. But the well-documented privacy issues with Google may prove a deterrent for some users.

Users trying to select a tool might spend a few days writing in each one, exporting and/or copying and pasting their work into Word, and deciding which is the easiest to use and which is the easiest to convert. Even if one doesn't stick with a tool, the words, if not the formatting, can still be easily moved into another web-based tool or client-based word processor.

Whether collaborative or solitary, writing is ultimately about the words. These cloud-based tools are not necessarily going to make ideas come more quickly, but they are designed to make the words easier to get down.

6

Staying organized

Abstract: Organization is a key part of the research process. After all, what good are amazing discoveries and brilliant writing if deadlines are constantly being missed. This is especially important for junior faculty and beginning researchers, who may not have the established body of work that can engender forgiveness and extensions for better-known, experienced researchers. This chapter will explore cloud-based organization tools, ranging from the conceptually simple, such as web-based calendars, to more complex project management tools such as Basecamp and Trello. It will also discuss robust to-do list applications, such as Remember the Milk, Google Tasks, and Asana. The productivity subculture around OS X will also be explored. The chapter will also provide a framework for how to think about productivity tools and what qualities users might wish to consider when evaluating a tool.

Key words: Asana, Basecamp, calendars, Google Tasks, organization, OS X, productivity, Remember the Milk, Trello.

Time management is an often-overlooked aspect to academia. Ultimately, reading, writing and researching do not mean much if deadlines are missed. Academics tend to think of time management as an undergraduate issue. The reality is more and more academics have more and more on their plate, making it increasingly it easier for responsibilities, like deadlines, to get lost in the shuffle.

Research is a process and processes require steps. Many users have a system for keeping track of what they need to do next and when it needs to be done, but, anecdotally, it seems there are quite a few researchers who struggle with the logistics of keeping track of research, deadlines, and next steps.

For researchers who struggle with staying organized, there are many cloud-based tools that can help them stay on-task. Some users might wonder what the cloud can provide that a good paper calendar or to-do list cannot. Other than persistent access across devices, something that paper cannot do the second a user leaves a list or calendar behind is remind users it is time to do something. Reminder functionality is a key feature for users trying to make sure they do not forget something important.

Staying organized is a complex act. It depends on a lot of variables, most significantly, the temperament of the person trying to stay organized. Unfortunately, there is no one tool or process that will work for every user. Instead, users should think about what is effective in their current work flow and what might be lacking. Armed with that information, they can review the tools described in this chapter and cherry pick the services that might address a need.

Web-based calendars

Web-based calendars, at their most basic, are calendars that are available from the web at any time. Users can consult the calendar to see where they need to be at any moment. Web-based calendars are a fairly standard component of most email services. Hotmail (transitioning into the name Outlook. com) offers one (*calendar.live.com/*) (Figure 6.1), as do Yahoo! (*calendar.yahoo.com/*), AOL (*calendar.aol.com/*), Zoho

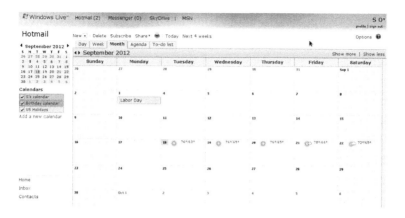

Figure 6.1 Outlook calendar

(*calendar.zoho.com/mycalendar*) and Google (*calendar. google.com*). There are also standalone calendar sites, such as 30Boxes (*30boxes.com/*). Many enterprise email systems, such as Microsoft Exchange and Novell GroupWise, also have a web-based calendaring component.

Rather than describe each of those specific calendar tools, this chapter will discuss features active researchers might find helpful in terms of staying on top of their work. It will also suggest some ways to use web-based calendars to stay organized.

In terms of selecting a web-based calendar, users might want to begin with what they already have access to. A convenient place to begin the exploration is with a user's current email provider, where some sort of calendaring service is probably already provided.

If a user is committed to checking their calendar daily, the calendaring process is simple – simply enter in what needs to be done and the date by which the task needs to be completed. However, one thing to consider is the due date of a project versus the possible duration of a project.

For example, if a completed manuscript is due 1 June, the user might toggle to the 1 June box of their calendar and enter "manuscript due." But if the manuscript has yet to be written, and the user does not see that a manuscript is due until the day it is due, then the calendar has failed the user. So one approach to calendars might be to budget the time needed before a project is due. In the example here, if the user knows a manuscript might take a week to complete, they might want to make a calendar entry one week before 1 June, reminding them to begin the project before it is due, with enough time to complete the project.

Another approach, alluded to earlier in this chapter, is to make use of the reminder functionality available in many web-based calendars. The reminder functionality allows users to be notified about an event, with the option to select when they want to be reminded. So in the 1 June example, if the user knows they'll need a week to complete the manuscript, they can enter the 1 June due date on 1 June and request a reminder one week before. The reminder is usually sent to an email account, although some, like Google's calendar, also allow notifications to be sent to mobile devices.

Many of these web-based calendars, such as the Outlook. com calendar, will also integrate with client-based calendar software, such as the myriad available for Android and iOS, as well as those that are desktop based, such as Mozilla's Lightning (*addons.mozilla.org/en-US/thunderbird/addon/ lightning/*), a plugin that brings calendar functionality to the Mozilla Thunderbird email client (*www.mozilla.org/en-US/ thunderbird/*). But perhaps the most famous desktop calendar client is OS X's iCal (now called Calendar), which can be synced against the cloud via iCloud, but also works with Google and Yahoo! calendars.

Integrating calendars with clients is not always simple, but for users who want their calendar available in multiple places and wish to use a client, there is usually a way to sync calendars, although not all web-based calendars can be updated via a client. What that means is that users will be able to see their calendars from multiple devices, but, depending upon the client and subscription method they are using, they might not be able to update their calendar from anything other than the calendar's web interface.

Take the Outlook.com calendar as an example. If the user wants to use a client, like iCal, to view their calendar rather than using the web interface, they will first have to make their calendar public. That means publishing it to the free web, where it is probably still relatively private via the principle of security through obscurity. Once the calendar is published, Outlook.com will offer the user an iCalendar feed of their calendar. That feed, an **.ics** file, can then be imported into iCal. All events from the Outlook.com calendar will show up on the iCal calendar, but the user will be unable to update their Outlook.com calendar via iCal. Changes will have to be made directly to the Outlook.com web calendar. The iCal subscription option is seen in many web-based calendars, including Yahoo!'s and Google's. It requires users to make their calendars public, since a feed cannot be grabbed if it is not public. Users can also usually subscribe to iCal feeds from within their calendars, too, so they can subscribe to a Google calendar from within a Yahoo! one, although, as with the client, they would not be able to update a non-native calendar.

Users looking to write to a web-based calendar using a client might have to do some research. The **CalDAV** standard makes that functionality possible and is supported by some web-based calendars, including Google and Yahoo!.

Once a client is configured, users can then get reminders on their desktop computers or on their mobile devices. They need to consider which represents the best method of being notified about an upcoming deadline.

Users looking to select a calendar might also consider whether they will be using the calendar alone or whether they will be sharing it with other users. Most web-based calendars now have some kind of sharing functionality where users can share calendars with each other, as long as they are all using the same web-based calendar platform. For instance, Google users can easily share calendars with other Google calendar users. Google has the added functionality of using shared calendars to schedule a meeting time when the other calendars involved in the meeting report open time slots. This functionality is also seen in enterprise solutions such as Outlook and GroupWise. It can be a huge time-saver when trying to schedule a meeting or a phone call. But like all calendars, it depends upon all parties being diligent about inputting their meetings and busy slots.

Web-based calendars also offer the ability to make recurring appointments, so if a user needs to remember to do something regularly for a project, they can make it a recurring appointment that will automatically appear on the calendar at the indicated intervals.

Many web-based calendars allow users to enter day-long events, which usually appear at the top of the daily calendar. This can be a useful way to keep track of events that need to happen by a certain day, but not by a certain time. For some, it can just provide an overall view of what needs to be accomplished in a given day, without specific times assigned to specific tasks. This type of calendaring dovetails with the work of David Allen, whose productivity book *Getting Things Done* is very popular in certain online circles, with many sites, tools, and apps dedicated to maintaining the principles outlined in the book. Essentially, Allen advocates keeping everything that needs to be done on a list and then constantly reviewing the list. His system does make room for calendars, but not as the primary organizational tool

(Allen, 2001: 94). If a user is specifically interested in implementing a *Getting Things Done* methodology, they should be prepared to augment their calendar tool in some way.

Web-based calendars offer many advantages over their paper-based counterparts. But perhaps the greatest advantage is in their ability to allow users to easily change things around. With a paper calendar, if a task does not get done, it needs to be moved to the next day. This is not uncommon for tasks that need to be done but are not urgent. With paper, tasks like that are constantly crossed out on one day and then moved to another one. If a user forgets to transfer a task, it could get lost. With web-based calendars, the process is much easier. At the end of the day a user can just drag any uncompleted tasks to the next day, with no erasing or crossing-out required.

All of the tools discussed in this section are free, as are many other (but not all) web-based calendars.

Remember the Milk

Remember the Milk (*www.rememberthemilk.com/*) is a cross between a to-do list and a calendar (Figure 6.2). Users begin typing to create a new task. The task is then on the user's list. Tasks can have due dates or be open-ended. They can also be postponed. It's a simple service made useful by a few key functions that go beyond a simple checklist of things that need to be done. One of the functions that makes Remember the Milk so useful is the way it integrates with other tools and technologies.

Users can integrate it with Gmail and Google Calendar. This allows them to view Remember the Milk tasks while they are doing something else, like checking email. Remember the Milk can also be integrated with Outlook and BlackBerry,

Figure 6.2   Remember the Milk

but not on the free tier. In general, the service strives to figure out a way to bring a user's to-do list to wherever the user might want to view it or add to it. For instance, every task in Remember the Milk provides an iCalendar link, which can be used to import the task into a web- or client-based calendar. This allows users to import tasks into an interface they might prefer to Remember the Milk. Each task also has its own RSS feed, so users can track their tasks through an RSS reader, if that is easier for them. Success using Remember the Milk does not necessarily hinge on using the site's web interface. There is enough integration across tools and services to make it more of a personal productivity data source than a singular web experience.

Another aspect to Remember the Milk that is useful is the structure of the entries. Remember the Milk entries can be as simple as the task to be accomplished, with no additional data. But users can also enter additional information, making their planning as detailed as makes sense to them. Users can tag their tasks, and assign URLs and locations. They can also estimate the amount of time a task will take. Notes can be attached to tasks and tasks can be prioritized.

Users can group tasks in tabs, perhaps separating work, research, and home. Remember the Milk has global reminder settings, so users can configure it to send reminders when a task is due, or a certain period of time before it is due. It can also send daily reminders for what is due each day.

Remember the Milk has an interesting function called Smart Lists, where users can create lists based upon criteria such as the appearance of certain keywords, when the task is due, or how often it has been postponed.

All of this functionality makes Remember the Milk more of a platform than a calendar. Where a calendar is date focused, Remember the Milk is task focused, and conceptually that can make a big difference to some users.

Remember the Milk also has the ability to add contacts, allowing users to share tasks. This requires that a contact become a member of Remember the Milk. Users can send tasks to contacts, which could make for a convenient work flow for people collaborating on a project.

Remember the Milk has clients for Android and iOS, making it easy for users to track tasks from anywhere. It is free, but offers a "Pro" service tier for $25 per year. The Pro tier gives users access to certain services, such as the Outlook and BlackBerry features mentioned earlier. It also gives users access to priority support and to mobile clients with more features than the free versions.

Basecamp

Basecamp (*basecamp.com/*) is project management software seemingly designed for small companies, so it does not perfectly translate to academics (Figure 6.3). But there is a lot of overlap in how both types of groups need to collaborate and adhere to a schedule.

Figure 6.3 Basecamp

Basecamp has quite a few areas, so there is a learning curve to it, but for users collaborating on a project, especially a complex project, it could be worth the time investment. It should also be noted that Basecamp is not free. The cheapest plan is $1 per day for 15 projects and 4 GB of storage. There is also a Personal tier that is a flat $25 per project. However, the service comes with a two-month free trial, which should be enough time for most users to decide if it's worth the time and financial investments.

Once a user has created a Basecamp account and a Basecamp project, they can invite other users to participate in the project. Basecamp has a discussion area where users can track conversations asynchronously. Some users might find this helpful as the discussion area is an easy and public way for collaborators to communicate. Where an email might eventually become misplaced, the discussion area is in a static location within Basecamp.

Users can also create simple documents, presumably for note-taking and note-tracking purposes. These documents can be commented on, helpful if collaborators are trying to achieve some sort of consensus. One interesting element to Basecamp is just about every feature, from calendar events to to-do tasks, can be commented upon. Even users who are not a part of a Basecamp project can be temporarily "looped in." This feature allows a Basecamp user to post a discussion topic and include the email address of someone who needs to respond, but is not a member of the Basecamp project. The looped-in user will get an email with the discussion prompt. When the user responds to the email, their answer will be posted in the Basecamp discussion area. This maintains privacy within Basecamp while still allowing people outside a project to contribute their knowledge. Users associated with a project can also email content into Basecamp using a special email address associated with the project. Basecamp will email the user a confirmation that the content has been submitted and will then send the submitter a link that allows them to announce the new content to all, some, or no project members.

One of the more intriguing elements to Basecamp is its to-do lists, which can be assigned to specific users, much like Remember the Milk allows users to send tasks to each other. Items on the to-do list can also be given due dates.

Basecamp has a calendar for shared events and the ability to send reminders the morning of events. To-do list items with due dates will also show up on the Basecamp calendar. Users can also set their own reminder preferences, including whether to receive daily summary emails about what is happening with a given project.

The Basecamp process seems complicated, but the service does a nice job of making everything as simple as possible. One of the nicest features of Basecamp is the Me view, which shows everything a user did within a project that day, plus any to-do items assigned to the user. This presents a nice summary of what the user has done within Basecamp, although, obviously, activity outside Basecamp will not show up unless it was tied to an activity within Basecamp. So the usefulness of the view depends upon how much work is documented within Basecamp. There is also a Daily Progress view, which shows what everyone involved in a project did in a given day, but which, like the Me view, depends upon how committed users are to documenting all project steps within Basecamp. Basecamp also has project templates, so once a user has a Basecamp setup that's effective, they can easily repeat it across new projects.

Basecamp is not for everyone, but for users who are committed to taking advantage of its various functionalities (including integration with many third-party services), it could represent a relatively simple way to track complex projects. However, it is also worth noting that users could probably replicate much of Basecamp's functionality using tools like a web-based calendar and some sort of task manager like Google Tasks or Remember the Milk.

There is nothing stopping an individual from using Basecamp without collaborators, but much of the value of the tool seems to come from using it to track what others are doing.

Google Tasks

There are many online to-do lists that allow users to create a simple task list and check things off as the items are accomplished. There are also many to-do list clients for mobile devices, and ways to manage a to-do list via the cloud without relying on a specific application. For instance, users can use any number of cloud-based word processors and/or writing tools to keep a list of things that need to be done. When a task is accomplished, the item can simply be removed from the list or marked with a special character. Users interesting in managing a to-do list solely from a mobile device can explore a myriad of options and pick whichever seems most pleasant to work with. But for users looking for something a bit more robust, and something that is easy to manage from desktops and mobile devices, Google Tasks is worth exploring (Figure 6.4).

Google Tasks is a Google service that works across Gmail and Google Calendar. It's not a stand alone service per se, although a user who has created a Google Task list can view it as a standalone service at *mail.google.com/tasks/ig?pli=1*. But the more traditional way to access Tasks is via Google Calendar, where it shows up as Tasks in one of the user's calendars. Clicking the *Tasks* link brings up a to-do list within the Google Calendar interface. Users can manage their list via the Google Calendar view and can add Gmail messages as tasks via the Gmail More option. This functionality is most valuable to researchers using Gmail and/or Google Calendar and/or iGoogle, as the cross-service integration puts the tasks in a number of places, where the list is always visible, helping to keep researchers focused on what needs to be accomplished next. Google Tasks also allows users to create sublists, which allows for detailed project management. Even non-Google users might find some value in Google Tasks, if for nothing else than as a place to begin experimenting with cloud-based to-do lists.

Figure 6.4   Google Tasks

There are third-party Google Tasks interfaces for iOS and Android. There are also browser extensions for the Chrome and Firefox browsers.

Trello

Trello (*www.trello.com*) is a visual way to track a project (Figure 6.5). It uses a board metaphor for organizing information, much the way many people organize projects on physical boards. Each virtual board can have virtual cards added. The cards are tasks, but can be filled out with more information, such as due dates and file attachments. Cards can also be assigned to other Trello members, making it another useful platform for collaboration. Users can subscribe to individual cards, comment upon them, and even upvote ideas, allowing project members to also communicate within the interface. Trello also allows users to create organizations, which are groups with members. This is another tool that could be helpful for users working as part of a team. Trello also has a notification and activity area that lets users know what's been happening with a project.

Figure 6.5   Trello

As with Basecamp, this is most effective if users document activities within Trello. Cards can also have checklists attached to them, allowing users to track smaller projects within the larger one. It creates a flow of boards comprised of cards and cards comprised of lists. Users can drill down into the part of the project they wish to tackle next.

The visual nature of Trello makes it fairly simple to use. Users click on cards and are presented with options. Cards can be moved around very easily. The ability to upload files is helpful for academics, who might want to attach article PDFs to cards. Users of a certain age might be used to doing research using index cards, with each index card representing an idea to be used in a larger work, and with the index cards arranged by potential chapter or section. Trello is an electronic way to use this same workflow. Files can be uploaded from a local machine, but also via Dropbox and Google Drive.

Trello is free, although there is a paid business class tier that probably would not be helpful to most researchers. Trello has an Android and iOS app and a mobile interface for users without the app.

Asana

Asana is a relatively new service developed by one of Facebook's founders (Hardy, 2012) (Figure 6.6). It is a team-based to-do list but it could also work for an individual. It's similar to Remember the Milk in that it allows users to create items that may or may not have a due date. Like Remember the Milk, it also allows users to assign priorities to tasks and to postpone items that don't need to be tackled right away.

117

Figure 6.6 Asana

While Asana is fine for someone to use alone, its strength is in its ability to help people collaborate. Users can assign tasks to each other, and can let others follow tasks so they know when an item is completed. Users can comment on tasks and email tasks into Asana. Users can also tag items, making it easy to see everything across projects. For instance, if a user was using Asana to manage multiple writing projects, they could tag all revision-related tasks with a tag such as "revise." Then, by searching the tag "revise," they could see all of the revision-related tasks across various projects.

Users can sync Asana due dates to their calendar using a calendar subscription feed. This allows them to see Asana due dates within their own calendar interfaces.

Because Asana is such a new service, it's difficult to predict how much traction it has and what its long-term prospects are. The interface is very responsive, feeling more like software than a web page, and while there is a bit of a learning curve, users will soon find it very simple to add and delegate tasks, and many will appreciate the ability of Asana to give users an overview not just on what they themselves need to do, but also to let everyone working on a project see what needs to be done, and by whom.

Asana is free but has premium tiers. For most academics who are not conducting massive projects with lots of people, the free, basic tier should be more than robust enough.

Mac productivity

As has been alluded to a few times already in this chapter, there are many corners of the Internet devoted to the concept of personal productivity. The website Lifehacker (*lifehacker. com/*) probably represents the nexus of these conversations, even though that site has expanded beyond work-based productivity into broader areas such as diet and exercise. Within the world of personal productivity sites, there is an even more specific subset of users discussing the topic from a purely OS X/iOS perspective. Many of these users are also heavily influenced by David Allen's (2001) *Getting Things Done* methodology. The website 43 Folders (*www.43folders. com/*), whose title comes from a *Getting Things Done* concept, used to be the center for many of these conversations, although that site is now irregularly updated.

To fully and effectively delve into the world of Mac productivity would require its own book. Users interested in extensively exploring the world of Mac productivity might want to look at books like those by David Sparks, *iPad at Work* (2011a) and *Mac at Work* (2011b). Sparks regularly writes about productivity for OS X/iOS users and has a website with a lot of freely accessible content: *www. macsparky.com/*.

Within the Mac productivity conversations, two pieces of software regularly come up: OmniFocus and Things. Neither has a Windows or Linux version, although there are somewhat comparable alternatives for both platforms.

OmniFocus (*www.omnigroup.com/products/omnifocus/*) is an incredibly robust to-do list manager that seems infinitely configurable (Figure 6.7). The desktop version is $79, the iPhone version is $19.99, and the iPad version is $39.99, so a user looking to use this across multiple devices could wind up with a steep price tag, depending upon the number of devices used.

Things (*culturedcode.com/things/*) is another task manager, this one costing $49.99 for the desktop version, $19.99 for the iPad version, and $9.99 for the iPhone one (Figure 6.8). Like OmniFocus, Things can be synced across devices.

An obvious question about the two tools is what differentiates them. The most significant differences are the interfaces. Users interested in exploring either of these tools will probably want to take advantage of the free trial each

Figure 6.7   OmniFocus

Figure 6.8 Things

tool offers and see which interface works best for their workflow. An interesting wrinkle is that each tool has multiple interfaces, depending upon the device on which it is being used. If a user does not like the iPad interface of one of the tools, but enjoys the desktop interface, deciding whether to move to that piece of software might be a more challenging decision.

Conceptually, both adhere to the *Getting Things Done* methodology, with tasks given contexts, rather than existing within a free-floating list. Both tools are flexible enough to be useful to users who do not practice or have never heard of *Getting Things Done*.

Conclusion

Organization is a complex task. Many users want a tool that will make them organized, but a tool can only do so much for a user. In the end, for a user to become organized, they must simply make more effort to do it themselves. So while none of the tools discussed in this chapter will magically and effortlessly make a disorganized user more organized, all of them can be used to help a disorganized user to become more organized, assuming they are willing to commit to consistently using a tool.

That is why the first step in choosing a tool to help a user become more organized should probably involve some self-reflection. The user needs to understand their weaknesses in order to select a tool that will compensate for those weaknesses.

For instance, many users seem to sign up for services, spend some time playing with them, perhaps even starting to create a workflow, and then forget about the service. If a user recognizes they are prone to forgetting to visit sites regularly, email or SMS/text reminders are a good way to couch that risk. The reminders provided by some of the services described in this chapter can keep users organized by delivering information to them, rather than depending on them to come to the information.

Of course, even the efficacy of reminders depends upon users entering the information somewhere and configuring a reminder to be sent. But even before a reminder can be configured, users need to think about deadlines that need to be met. Receiving an email that major article revisions are due the next morning is not as helpful as receiving that same kind of email a month before the major revisions are due.

Conversely, some users prefer to work with all of their information in a centralized place, without being notified of what needs to be done and by when. This is what some might call the to-do list methodology, where users have a list of things that need to be accomplished. Usually, the list is kept near the user's work space and they consult the list throughout the day, or even just once a day, to see what needs to be done. Many users work quite effectively with this kind of workflow. The advantage to using a cloud-based service for this sort of thing is that users always have access to the list, even when they are away from their usual work space.

Users looking for a centralized organizational solution should also factor in their mobile device. Many of the services discussed here have mobile versions of some sort. Given that many lists are not that complicated, it's perfectly viable to review the list from a mobile device rather than a desktop computer. That could make the mobile experience more important than the desktop one.

Users should also consider how many other people will depend upon an organizational tool. If someone is trying to organize a complex project, with multiple collaborators, something like Basecamp might be needed to make sure everyone is meeting their goals. But a simple project for someone working alone probably does not call for that level of complexity.

Users working to organize a team should also consider the comfort and skill levels of collaborators. A shared, web-based calendar can be challenging if users are all using different web-based calendars. But if someone knows how to export and import public calendar feeds, the prospect becomes a bit more viable.

Finally, when thinking about an organizational tool to adopt, users might consider cost, to a certain extent. For many users, free is often the preferred cost for a cloud-based service. But many of the organizational tools discussed in this chapter lack an easy and comprehensive way to export data. Most web-based calendars allow users to export their data, but depending upon the file size and the configuration of their calendars, importing the data into another tool is often a complex and ultimately time-consuming task. Once a user chooses an organizational tool, they probably do not want to have to leave it.

This is where cost can be a variable to consider. When a user chooses a free tool, they should consider whether the tool has a good chance of being around in a year – or in two years. Maciej Ceglowski, the founder of Pinboard (see Chapter 2), wrote an interesting blog post pointing out that many projects that are cost-free to end-users are often not sustainable over the long-term (see Chapter 9 for a further discussion of this). For data that is relatively portable, this represents a minor inconvenience, but for the type of data discussed in this chapter, the inconvenience might be considerably more severe. For instance, Remember the Milk allows users to export their data, but the data is in the form of an iCal file. How does one convert that iCal file back into one's notes? How long might that conversion take?

This is not to say that paid services are inherently more reliable than free ones. Rather, it is to point out that when a user pays for a service, they have some recourse if the service goes offline. With free services, there often is no recourse.

However, for users on a budget, or for users working with a simple organizational process, like a basic list of next steps, it is not always horribly challenging to re-create the functionality of paid tools using free ones. For instance, Asana and Trello are conceptually similar to Basecamp, providing users with a simple way to track projects. Users who like Basecamp, but who find the personal tier too limiting or expensive, might consider experimenting with one of the free tools.

Things and OmniFocus, two of the OS X/iOS productivity tools mentioned, have beautiful interfaces. But users might want to trial both tools to see how much of the advanced functionality they require for their work. Some users might discover they are able to track their work just as easily using a web-based document in something as simple as Yahoo! Notepad (see Chapter 5).

Also, by focusing on functionality rather than tools, users might find an organizational tool that was not intended to be one. Many of the web-based word processors discussed in Chapter 5, like the aforementioned Yahoo! Notes, would serve as a fine base for keeping one's work organized.

Also, some of the capture tools discussed in Chapter 2, especially the more robust ones, such as Springpad and Evernote might be useful for keeping a researcher, and their work, organized.

Ultimately, users must know themselves before they can commit to an organizational tool.

7

Communicating

Abstract: Web-based communication is an important aspect of academic life. Most users are probably familiar with email, but might have trouble managing it, as more and more communication has been pushed to email. However, there are other ways for users to communicate. This chapter will explore some of those tools, which include instant messaging services, such as those provided by AOL, Google, Yahoo!, Facebook, and Microsoft. It will also discuss clients which allow users to communicate across multiple chat services. Video chat services, such as Skype and Google+, will also be explored. This chapter will additionally discuss Internet Relay Chat, an older method of synchronous text-based communication that still has applications today, and will also address strategies for managing email.

Keywords: AIM, chat, instant messaging, Internet Relay Chat, Skype, video chat, Yahoo! Messenger.

Collaboration is an increasingly important aspect of the day-to-day life of academics, not just from committee work and teaching perspectives, but also from a scholarship and publishing one. For users to collaborate, they need to communicate.

It is no longer a given that users within close physical proximity will communicate face-to-face. For many, both within and outside academia, communication means email, although there are still pockets of users who prefer to communicate via telephone or face-to-face. And, of course, for users who are not proximate, email remains an ever important communication tool.

Email and telephone are fine methods of communication, but there are many other tools available if users are looking to get more out of their communications with colleagues, or if they are just looking to escape the deluge of email that seems to plague professionals around the world. This chapter will explore some of the tools that could make users' communication more productive, or, at the very least, provide some new ways to effectively communicate with colleagues across the globe and across the hall.

Managing email

Most users are familiar with email. The utility of it is that it allows users to deal with requests on their own schedule, where telephone calls can be more intrusive. Email is also useful because a user's inbox might serve as a list of things that need to be done. That same utility often becomes a downfall as users become overwhelmed by the quantity of emails in their inbox, with important messages pushed to the bottom of the email screen as new messages come in.

This section will not review email services or clients, as they are all largely the same. Instead, it will offer some suggestions for using a current email service more effectively. Users feeling overwhelmed by email might consider exploring some of the organizational tools discussed in Chapter 6, which would allow them to move or delete emails as tasks are moved from an email inbox into a particular tool.

Those overwhelmed by email might consider using folders (or labels, in the parlance of Gmail) as a way to keep their inbox clean. There are many theories on how to best process email. Some users prefer detailed folders/labels to make it easier to find older messages. Other theories recommend using fewer folders, making email more about action and less about sorting. One theory advocates three folders: "follow up," for messages that require additional steps; "archive," for messages requiring no action, but that the user might need to consult at another point; and "hold," for messages users will be working with in the short term (Trapani, 2006). The three-folder theory is based upon a five-folder theory that recommends: a "respond" folder, for items requiring a quick response; "action," for items requiring detailed follow-up; "hold," for items that might be consulted in the next few days; "waiting," for items waiting for a response from someone else; and "archive," for messages that are no longer needed but might need to be consulted later (Mann, 2005). Merlin Mann has written extensively about email management, even coining the phrase "inbox zero," which refers to the idea of effectively processing emails to the extent that they do not accumulate in an inbox. Mann's articles on the concept can be found at *inboxzero. com/articles/*.

This is but a tiny drop of the work available in the bucket of email management. Users looking for a process might read around and see which systems or processes make sense. The idea is not to spend hours organizing email, but to be able to retrieve needed messages quickly and to keep track of tasks that need to be accomplished. For some, that means leaving everything in an inbox and constantly reviewing messages. For others, it means exporting information out of email and into tools like calendars and task managers (see Chapter 6). Others might find one of the aforementioned limited folder organization methods effective. The issue is not best practices in general so much as it is what works best for the individual.

One final issue to consider around email folders is the search ability of Gmail. Users have gravitated toward filing email into folders because, historically, email search has been both slow and bad. Gmail changed that, though, with a search precise enough that users who use labels purely for the sake of being able to easily retrieve messages later might find that the Gmail search can replace the email filing process.

Other theories of email organization discuss the role of automated filters in processing email (Strohmeyer, 2011). An email filter, often called a rule, is a logic created within an email program that allows mail to be routed based upon certain parameters. Most users are probably familiar with the vacation rule, used for when someone is out of the office for an extended time period. The vacation rule sends an automatic response to an email, letting the sender know the intended recipient is out of the office, often explaining when the recipient will be back. But rules can also be used to automatically file certain types of email, or to automatically forward certain emails to other accounts. Users can take advantage of this functionality to process some of the emails they might be handling manually. For instance, many users, but especially librarians, it seems, participate on listservs. Depending upon the volume of the listserv, keeping up with it can be a daunting task. But a simple rule could route all listserv messages into a listserv folder (or label), so the user does not need to manually file emails. Every email program and service has a slightly different rule/filter creation mechanism, but, in general, they allow users to identify certain types of email, using a certain subject, sender, or recipient, or a key word combination. Once the email is identified, the second part of the rule/filter creates an action for emails that match the first part of the rule/filter. So for the listserv example, the rule/filter might have all emails with a subject that matches the subject of a certain listserv filed immediately into a folder/label for that listserv. For the end-user, it means the email will never actually appear in their inbox. Instead, they can just periodically check the folder to catch up on listserv messages, perhaps using one of the aforementioned calendars or to-do lists to remind them to regularly check the folder.

Filters can be an effective way of handling unimportant email – the items that users want to be informed about, but do not necessarily need to track in a specific timeframe. But they can also be used to forward messages to other email accounts. Many users have multiple email accounts. One might be a work email account and another might be a personal account. One might be checked more regularly than the other. Users worried about missing important messages might set up a rule to forward important emails (importance could be determined using a list of known important senders, or perhaps any email coming from a certain domain) sent to a less frequently checked account to a more frequently checked one. This can be taken a step further, with forwarded emails sent from a less frequently checked email account automatically routed into a special folder or flagged as important (different email clients and services have different ways for users to do this) when they arrive in the more regularly checked account.

Filters can take some time to set up, but for certain users, especially those dealing with a lot of email that doesn't regularly require personal action, they can be an effective way to keep an inbox under control.

Finally, while not viable for most users, another approach to an overwhelming amount of email is to file for email bankruptcy. Author and academic Lawrence Lessig coined the term in 2004 upon realizing he would not be able to catch up on the email he had accumulated. He sent a note out to everyone who had sent him an email to which he had not yet replied, informing them he would not be able to do so, and asking them to re-send their email if they still needed a response (Fitzgerald, 2004). Most users will not be able to declare email bankruptcy, but perhaps the fact that the idea seems attractive at all might inspire some to institute some organization to their email practices. This idea might be especially intriguing in light of a recent study that found workers who were taken off email were less stressed and more productive than workers with email (Bilton, 2011). While it is hard to imagine any academic institution would discontinue email, the study does illustrate the toll email takes on people.

Instant messaging

Readers of a certain age might have some fond memories of logging into America Online, an early dial-up Internet provider now known as AOL, and using the AOL chat tool, which would eventually be called AOL Instant Messenger, or **AIM** (*www.aim.com/*) (Figure 7.1). Online chatting involves typing messages to another user in real-time. AIM is just one of the instant messaging (often abbreviated **IM**) tools now available to users.

Most chat services (Google, Yahoo!, Facebook, Skype, and Microsoft are but a few of the many companies offering some kind of chat service) are not completely interoperable, meaning that if a user has an account on one service, it is not a given they will be able to chat with users on another. For instance, users of Yahoo! Messenger (*messenger.yahoo. com/*), Yahoo!'s chat client (Figure 7.2), can communicate with other Yahoo! users and with users of the Facebook chat service, but not with AIM users.

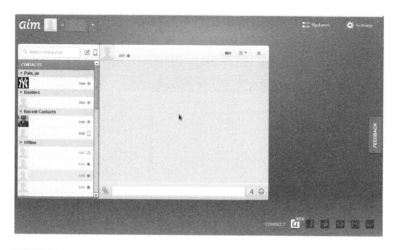

Figure 7.1 AIM

Instant messaging represents an intriguing way to communicate because of its immediacy, but also, because of how well it can also work asynchronously. If a user has a question for a colleague, they can send an instant message. If the colleague is available and can answer the question, they type the response. If the colleague is unavailable, they can answer the question when they return to their desk, or if they are online somewhere else, as most chat services can be accessed on mobile devices. Because instant messages tend to pop up on screens, they are often more immediate than email. Two users online at the same time can quickly "discuss" an issue. Most instant messaging services allow users to indicate their status, so if a user is online but working on something else, they can indicate they are not available for chat at the moment. Users can also choose to sign out of chat when they are busy. For certain types of conversations, a telephone might be easier, but if users are exchanging text or links, chat can be a much quicker and easier way to trade information.

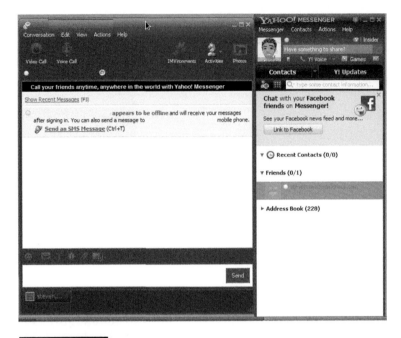

Figure 7.2 Yahoo! Messenger

Chat can also be easier to manage for users trying to keep their email inbox under control. Two colleagues trying to resolve something over email might generate five or six emails in a very short amount of time. Instant messages have that same kind of back-and-forth without adding to a user's inbox count.

Most chat services offer the same functionality, so in terms of choosing a service, users might begin with a service that their collaborators also use. Many email services have an instant messaging component. Yahoo! and Hotmail/Outlook users can use their email credentials to access the various instant messaging services each company provides. Gmail users automatically have a chat account that shows up on the left pane of Gmail, showing Google contacts who are currently logged into chat. Yahoo! has also integrated chat into its email area.

Chat can take place in many environments. Most services have their own chat client that users can download and install. But many services also have a web interface that allows a user to access the chat service via a web browser. And some services, like Facebook's chat, do not have a proprietary client, but instead are completely web based (although Facebook chat can be accessed from third-party clients).

For users who have contacts across services, though, there are options to help consolidate instant messaging so they not wind up with multiple clients open on their mobile device or desktop. There are also web-based services that perform a similar function, without users downloading software to their local machine.

Pidgin, which can be downloaded from *pidgin.im/*, is available for Windows, OS X, and Linux (Figure 7.3). It is a chat client that supports multiple services, including Yahoo!,

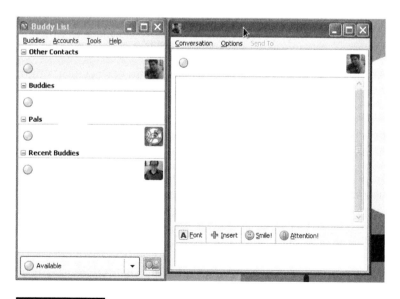

Figure 7.3 Pidgin

Windows Live, and Google Talk (also often referred to as Google Chat or gchat, and eventually to be replaced by Hangouts). It also supports Internet Relay Chat (**IRC**), which is discussed later in this chapter. Pidgin can support additional services, such as Facebook, with the use of plugins that are installed in the local client. Then, the user just needs to obtain credentials for all of the services they wish to use and enter them into the Pidgin client. Messages will all appear within the Pidgin interface, so a user can chat in one window with someone using Facebook chat and in another with a user using AIM. Pidgin provides a seamless experience for the user, regardless of the chat services in play. OS X users might wish to explore Adium (*www.adium.im*), which is similar to Pidgin.

For users who don't want to download a client, or who just need access to their instant messaging networks temporarily on a computer they do not normally use, there are many browser-based services that allow users to access multiple IM networks without having to download a client. Trillian for Web (*www.trillian.im/chat*) is one example of this kind of service, as are imo (*imo.im/*) and IM+ (*plus.im*). All three services allow users to create master accounts that remember all of their IM credentials across services, or to simply log into a single service using the web interface provided by the browser-based service.

Most instant messaging services now support video chat, which is discussed later in this chapter. Many also allow users to send files. Some even support chat rooms, which would allow more than two users at a time to chat. Instant messaging represents an often underused way for collaborators to quickly communicate across devices. Users in a situation where they constantly find themselves emailing colleagues and then waiting for a quick answer might be pleased with the responsiveness instant messaging provides.

Video chat

If IRC represents communication through a tool from the past, video chat represents the future. Where IRC and instant messaging use text for users to communicate, video chat allows users to see each other's faces and even to share desktop screens, creating a face-to-face experience, even when the faces are not in the same room with each other. Users wishing to use video chat will need a device with a web camera of some sort and, depending upon their hardware, might also need a microphone. Many recent laptops come with a built-in webcam, as do most modern phones. Like instant messaging, users need to be on the same network, or on a network that offers interoperability.

Google Talk and Yahoo! Messenger support video chat. Users already using those services might consider simply adapting the video chat features available in each of the clients. This might be the path of least resistance for someone looking to transition into video chat. Users without a web camera or microphone can find both inexpensively online. Users not concerned about the physical size of the camera will find more favorable pricing than users looking for the smallest possible camera.

Skype is a dedicated video call service that is based around the Skype client (Figure 7.4). Skype also supports audio calls and text chat. There are clients for Windows, OS X, Linux, Android, iOS, and Windows Phone, so it's widely available across platforms. There are a number of services available across its free tier, including free video calls. However, certain features, such as group video calls, require a $5 per month paid subscription. That is significant, because group video calls might be an important feature for users working with more than one collaborator. Skype also allows users to share files and to share desktop screens, which, depending upon the

Figure 7.4   Skype

nature of a collaboration, could be very helpful. It is worth mentioning that Facebook's video call service uses Skype.

Users interested in the idea of video conferencing, that is, using a video call with more than one other user, might want to explore Google Hangouts, a part of the Google+ social network (*plus.google.com/*). Google Hangouts allows more than one simultaneous video call partner, allowing a group of people to communicate using video. Google Hangouts also allows users to integrate Google Drive and to share screens from their desktop. Hangouts is available on Android and iOS devices via the Google+ app and can be launched from the Gmail interface. It is replacing Google Talk.

OS X users have Messages available to them. Messages, formerly known as iChat, is the OS X chat client and service. It supports text chat, video chat and group video chat. It also integrates with the iOS FaceTime service, which allows users to video chat from their iPhones and iPads.

When choosing a video chat tool, the first thing a user should consider is whether they'll want to communicate with more than one person at a time. Multiple-person video calls are possible via Skype, but require a paid subscription, where video calls are free from within Google+. So a user looking for group video must weigh the desire to use Skype against the desire to pay for Skype. OS X users have Messages available, but only if everyone involved in the video call has Messages.

Users who don't anticipate group video calls might consider sticking with their current instant messaging service and exploring the video chat options available with it, although not all video call service experiences are equal. Users might find some to be a bit slow to load and difficult to work with. If that is the case, they might explore another client or service, although, as with the text-based chat tools, users are limited by the tools and services used by their collaborators. If all of a user's colleagues use Yahoo! Messenger to communicate, it's probably not realistic to switch to Google Talk.

IRC

As mentioned previously, many instant messaging tools support some sort of group chat function but for users who regularly work with a large team, group instant messaging chat might not always be easy to implement. One interesting option to consider is IRC, an old-fashioned chat room protocol that is still very popular within certain communities, especially within open source software development.

IRC is accessed via special IRC servers. The servers are accessed via clients, although there are some browser add-ons that can bring IRC functionality to the browser. One is ChatZilla, which works with the Firefox browser (*chatzilla. hacksrus.com/*). Another is Mibbit webchat for the Chrome browser and which can be found in the Chrome Web Store. In terms of clients, Windows users can use mIRC which is a dedicated IRC client (*www.mirc.com/*). Users can evaluate it free for 30 days, but registering costs $20, which covers up to three home computers and all future mIRC releases. Colloquy (*colloquy.info/*) and Xirc (*www.aquaticx.com/*) are two free OS X IRC clients. XChat is the default IRC client on many Linux distributions, and is also available for Windows (*xchat.org/*) (Figure 7.5). Users looking to move into the world of IRC do not need to make a substantial financial investment in clients.

Upon launching most clients, users will be prompted to create a nickname. This is how their name will appear within IRC. IRC names must be unique, meaning if someone else on your server has your nickname, you must change yours. Many IRC servers allow users to register their nicknames so they always have the same nickname. Each IRC server is separate from others, so if you have a certain

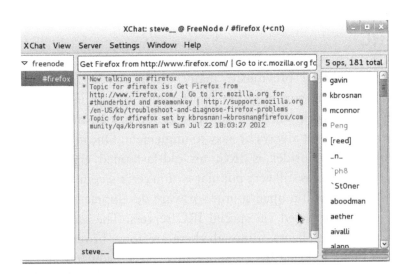

Figure 7.5 XChat

nickname on the Freenode servers, for example, you might not have that same nickname on another service unless you register that same nickname.

Once a user has selected a nickname, with many clients also asking users to suggest backup nicknames, users must choose a server on which to communicate. As mentioned previously, users cannot communicate across servers, so if someone is on Efnet servers and they want to speak with someone on IRCnet, it won't be possible through IRC.

After choosing a server, users must select a room. A room is just a space on an IRC server where a group of users can communicate. Anything typed in the room can be seen by anyone in the room, just like a face-to-face conversation. This is where IRC is very useful and this application is probably the most useful to academics. It allows a space for a group of users to easily communicate with each other simultaneously. This is also why it is so popular in software development. It is a quick and easy way for a group to communicate. Plus, because group conversations are recorded, it makes it very easy for users to catch up on what they might have missed. Someone can either create a transcript of what everyone said via simple copying and pasting, or can join a room and leave their client open, allowing them to see everything said in the room, even if they were looking at something else at the time it was written. Users can also send private messages and files to each other. The ability to send private messages provides options in terms of what is communicated publicly versus what is communicated privately.

There are two usage cases for IRC. One is where a user wishes to access an IRC space being used by someone else. The most likely occurrence of this case is if a user needs some sort of technical support and has been directed to access the support via IRC. In this usage case, the user will need the name of the IRC server and the name of the room where the support is provided. IRC room names are preceded by hashtags, so a room called researchproject would be referred to as #researchproject. This is similar to the way hashtags are used to describe content on Twitter, which is discussed in Chapter 8. The user will access their IRC client and use the option to connect to a server, selecting the server needed. Most clients allow users to add servers to the existing list, but most support comes through fairly well-known servers that should be listed within the client. Once a user is connected to a server, there should be a dialogue asking them to select the room they wish to join. After the user types in the room name they find themselves in the room, where they can interact with others there, taking note that IRC rooms have their own social norms and customs, which might seem foreign to outsiders. IRC also has standard commands that can be used. For instance, nicknames can be changed using the */nick* command followed by the new nickname. New rooms can be joined using the */join* command and the name of the room. But clients also provide menu-driven ways to accomplish these tasks.

The second usage case, and the one that will probably be more helpful, is where a user wants to create a space for others to work within. To do this, the user first selects a server and informs their collaborators of the name of the server. Freenode.net (*freenode.net/*) is a good server to use, as it supports many open source and non-profit projects. In terms of selecting a room, a user just needs to decide on a room name and then join it using the */join* command followed by *#nameofroom*. If the room does not exist, it will be created when the first person joins it. Any subsequent collaborators who type that same command, or use their client to join that room, will all be in the same room where the collaborators can then communicate with each other synchronously. Rooms are public, and anyone can join any room, but there is usually very little danger that someone will be interested in joining a relatively random room with a bunch of users discussing the same project. Freenode does allow groups to register channels, so they have persistent access to the same channel all the time. For most users working with known collaborators, this option is unnecessary.

Once users are up to speed on using IRC and navigating through their client, it represents a very quick and easy way for them to work together. There are certainly other tools that support group chat, but IRC is fast, cheap, and does not take up a lot of system resources. Some might consider IRC old fashioned, which it is. But it has survived because it is reliable and effective. Users can make a persistent work environment, registering nicknames (which is how the name will be displayed within the IRC environment) and reserving specific rooms on servers, but they can just as easily make it an ad hoc experience, with users grabbing nicknames and rooms as they need them and adjusting them if either is not available.

There are also mobile IRC clients available and, while it does not provide for an ideal mobile experience, it does allow users to synchronously collaborate on the go. IRC is an accessible space that also provides an easy way for users to document conversations. While there is a bit of a learning curve getting started with IRC, once users have everything set up, re-accessing the space is a matter of a few clicks or commands. IRC is no longer sexy but it is still a viable way for groups to communicate.

Conclusion

Effective communication, like effective organization, is complicated because it relies not just on technical tools, but also on the implementation of the tools. In general, it is probably best not to view these separate sections as mutually exclusive. Just as the invention of the telephone did not completely replace letters and the fax machine did not supplant the telephone, all of these communication tools can peacefully coexist. Users just need to consider what they need to communicate and how they might want the information communicated back to them. Then, they might think about the person they're communicating with and consider the most effective way to reach them, much the same way as academics consider the best journal for their type of research.

Some users are not responsive to email so it does not make sense to email them for something needed immediately. No amount of email management will get someone to respond when that is not their inclination. But perhaps introducing someone like that to chat might make them more reachable and responsive. The immediacy and impermanence of chat may represent an attractive alternative. Or, perhaps it is simply a matter of accepting that, for some users, a telephone is still the best way to get a response.

These tools are not answers so much as they're simply platforms. IRC is a fascinating and wonderful way for users to communicate, but all parties have to be committed to using it. This might require some social engineering, like perhaps a standing meeting that takes place within an IRC channel. Some users might have a more positive response to IRC if someone else configures their client for them. Little things like this make alternative means of communication more palatable to users who are not inclined to experiment.

And for users invested in Gmail, Google Hangouts is a fantastic tool, as it seamlessly integrates chat, both text and video, in the Gmail web interface. Emails and chat messages all wind up in the same place.

Finally, many organizations have their own chat tools, frequently based around the campus email system. If a user's campus or organization has access to this kind of tool, and if the user only needs to communicate with people within the campus or organization, this can be a simple and easy way to touch base, without having to investigate a new tool platform, although, like any new tool, there will probably be a learning curve in learning to use the enterprise chat tool.

There is no shortage of cloud-based communication options. The major challenge is getting collaborators to agree upon a tool and then to keep themselves in that magical middle ground, where communication is effective and robust, but no one feels inundated by messages.

8

Sharing

Abstract: The sharing of work has typically been a significant part of an academic life and career. Traditionally, sharing has meant formal outlets, such as peer-reviewed articles and conference presentations. However, there are other ways for work to be shared, using less formal channels. While these new channels might not be taken into consideration during the promotion and reappointment process, they still provide ways for academics to reach a broader audience and to hear feedback on their work that they might not receive in more formal sharing channels. This chapter will discuss those informal channels, covering blogs, both hosted and self-hosted, and microblogging sites, such as Tumblr and Twitter. The chapter will also discuss nameplate sites, which allow users to easily post a simple web page where they can share basic information about themselves and their work.

Key words: blog, microblog, nameplate, peer-review, sharing, Tumblr, Twitter.

Research is conducted with the goal of sharing results with a larger audience, usually in the form of some sort of formal work, such as a book, article, or presentation. But more and more academics are choosing to share their ideas in less formal arenas online. This occurs for many reasons. Some researchers enjoy the contact with the world outside the academy. Others appreciate the immediate feedback available when sharing online. Others see it as a networking opportunity, creating excitement and buzz around a research area. And some researchers participate in informal online arenas to be a part of the important conversations that take place away from formal academic publishing structures.

While it is impossible to truly capture all of the reasons why an increasing number of academics are choosing to share parts (or even all) of their work online, there is no denying that it is very much a trend. To see it, all one needs to do is search the Internet for the name of a discipline combined with a term like "blog" or "Twitter." For researchers who are curious about moving their work into a more public sphere, this chapter will provide an overview of the different electronic platforms that serve as informal channels, with the caveat that different organizations and institutions have their own policies and cultures regarding informal online sharing. Users should consider those cultures when choosing to share work in informal channels.

A final note about this chapter: it does not address sharing across social networks because of the size of the topic and because it is beyond the scope of the chapter. While all of the services discussed within this chapter have a social component, as one might expect within a chapter about sharing work, they all provide the opportunity to share content in a purely professional sense, without revealing any personal information. That kind of personal/professional separation is more challenging to implement in environments such as Facebook and Google+, which at their core, are personal sharing networks.

Blogs

The traditional definition of a blog is a frequently updated site with content appearing in reverse chronological order, with the most recent content appearing at the top of the page, and moving down the page as new content is added. Blogs have evolved into more of a content management system concept, where the display of the content is more flexible, and allows for the presentation of static content, like curriculum vitae (CVs) or personal statements. Users no longer need to think that having a blog means committing to regular updates. Instead, they might think of it as an easy way to create a web presence that does not require a lot of technical know-how. And of course, for users who do wish to regularly post content, blogs are still an excellent way to do so.

There are a variety of blog platforms, but before exploring the platforms, users must first consider the type of blog they wish to create – a hosted blog or a self-hosted one. Hosted blogs live on a server maintained by someone else. Most services give users a subdomain on their domain, so a user of the Blogger service would have a web address of *blogname*.blogger.com. However many blogging services also allow user to publish to their own domain, so if a user owns the domain *www.example.com*, they can use certain hosted services to publish to that domain without having to install or configure software on a server for which the user is responsible.

Self-hosted blogs require access to a server where software is installed and maintained by the user. One of the most popular platforms for this is WordPress (*www.wordpress.org*) (Figure 8.1). Self-hosted blogs provide a great degree of control and customization, but also require some degree of technical know-how and access to a server that meets the requirements of the blog software. Many web hosts provide access to the Softaculous Autoinstaller, which allows users to easily install software, including WordPress, from the control panel of their server. The user is still responsible for

Figure 8.1   WordPress

tasks such as backing up the blog and keeping software updated. For technical users or users interested in learning more about maintaining a web service, self-hosted blog software such as WordPress can be a rewarding experience. But users who do not wish to deal with any of these issues might be better off exploring the many hosted solutions available, with the understanding that the price of technical convenience is configurability. WordPress is free and open source, but users wishing to use it will probably have to pay for web hosting.

Users wishing to run a blog on their own servers might also explore Movable Type (*www.movabletype.com*), which is free for individuals and pre-kindergarten through 12th grade educational institutions. However, there is a charge for business and enterprise use. Users should be cautioned that the free version of Movable Type does not include support. Like WordPress, Movable Type is designed for users with a certain level of technical expertise, or for users who have access to people with a certain level of technical expertise. There are also many full-blown content management systems with blog functionality, such as Joomla (*www.joomla.org*), Drupal (*www.drupal.com*), and ExpressionEngine (*www.expressionengine.com*). Like Movable Type and WordPress, all of these would require server access to implement.

WordPress also provides a hosted platform for users (*www.wordpress.com*). The basic level is free, but additional features such as redirecting to a customized web address, extra storage, and customization, require annual fees. The basic hosted WordPress blog is sufficient to get most users started. Users requiring more functionality or customization can either purchase the additional features or move their hosted content onto a self-hosted instance of WordPress.

Blogger (*www.blogger.com*), was one of the first companies, if not the first, to offer hosted blogging services for users (Figure 8.2). It was eventually purchased by Google and is now part of Google's portfolio of services. Blogger offers no

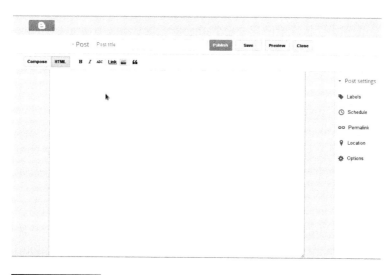

Figure 8.2   Blogger

premium services, but allows users to redirect content to a domain they own for free.

TypePad (*www.typepad.com*) is another hosted platform, created by the same team as behind the Movable Type server software. Unlike other hosted services discussed so far, TypePad is not free. There is a free trial, but pricing begins at $8.95 per month.

Users can find lots of other hosted services, but should be careful when selecting one. Because the user does not control the server where the software is hosted, it can often be hard to export content. If a service abruptly goes out of business, users could easily lose all of their content. While any service, especially a free one, can be canceled at any time, using a major service, like any of the ones described here, at least ensures the cancellation of the service will be met with some kind of large public outcry, as opposed to a minor service going out of business, where very few people might take note.

There are also quite a few blog platforms for servers. While the risk of data loss is diminished by the user having control of the entire server, support can vary from software to software, especially free and/or open source software. In addition to looking at the software itself, users should consider the community supporting the software. Something used by just a few people will probably not develop as quickly as a popular platform. Part of what has made WordPress such a popular platform is the community that supports it, improving the platform as well as creating plugins that add functionality to the basic software.

Users looking to start a blog might first begin with a hosted solution. Using a hosted solution allows a user to test-drive an interface before taking the trouble to download and configure software for a self-hosted blog. Users interested in playing with WordPress on a server might use the hosted version to get a feel for the software itself. Users interested in Movable Type might experiment with TypePad first.

In terms of features, users will find them fairly standard. Most blog platforms allow users to create a title and a post. Most platforms support tags and/or categories, as a way to describe content, as well as linking similar content together. Most platforms allow some degree of customization in terms of the look of the blog. Most also include some kind of statistical component, so a user can track traffic to their blog, seeing which posts are most popular and from which other sites they are receiving traffic.

Most platforms also support some kind of commenting functionality, which allows blog visitors to comment on content being posted. At its best, this can be a form of peer review, with users from around the world evaluating ideas, helping the blogger to refine their work, and perhaps even connecting with other researchers working on similar projects. At its worst, though, comments can be automated spam messages requiring a significant amount of time and energy to keep on top of. Across the board, blogging platforms, both hosted and self-hosted, are trying to solve the challenge of comments. Anything requiring too rigorous an authentication process tends to discourage users from posting comments. But making commenting too simple can invite a flood of low-quality and/or spam-like comments. One solution is to disable commenting, which most blog tools allow. Another option is to use a third-party service to implement and manage comments. One such solution is Comments Box (*developers.facebook.com/docs/reference/plugins/comments/*), which uses the Facebook credential as a way for users to post comments on content. Another tool is Disqus (*disqus.com*), which integrates with many blogging and microblogging platforms, allowing blog readers to post comments relatively easily, using a variety of credentials, including Facebook, Twitter, Yahoo!, Google, and OpenID, but also making it very easy for blog owners to moderate comments, using either the Disqus dashboard, or even just email.

Most blog tools also support collaboration, allowing more than one person to post content to a blog. For users working on a project together, this can represent an intriguing way to communicate either internally, via a password protected blog, or externally, as a public discussion of issues around the group research project.

As mentioned previously, most blog tools also support the creation of static pages, so even if users do not plan to create much new content, they can easily put up a few pages with information such as syllabi or class assignments. The ease with which blogs can be updated makes them an ideal way to manage a class. Some users might also use a blog as a personal repository of articles, with users posting versions of articles and chapters permitted by copyright. Users interested in the self-archiving rights permitted by the various journals might wish to consult RoMEO (*www.sherpa.ac.uk/romeo/*), a project that tracks journal self-archiving policies and makes them publicly available.

However, for many users, the public exchange of new ideas would probably be the main impetus behind a public blog, allowing researchers to share their work with an audience beyond that of an academic book or scholarly article. In the early days of the Internet, blogs were seen as a bit frivolous, almost like personal diaries posted for all to see. But now the format has gained mainstream acceptance, with blogs a part of every news organization's website, and a frequent part of professional organization sites, too. Blogs are no longer seen as vanity sites, but instead, are viewed as a means of quick and easy web-based communication with a broad audience.

Microblogs

Content exists on a continuum. At the far end would be a project like a book, which can take years to be written and published. Moving further down the continuum would be a scholarly article, which could take years, but, on the whole, would be expected to take less time than a book. Continuing down the continuum might be a blog post, which should take less time to compose than an article. And past the blog post on the content continuum? A microblog, which, like a blog, is a quick way to share content, but not necessarily to create it. Where blogs tend to contain original content (although not necessarily), microblogs tend to be a way to quickly share content created by others, whether the content is links, videos, or images. Microblogs are usually used to share content without much, if any, commentary.

For researchers, it presents an interesting space, where rather than writing about content, as they might be doing with a blog post, they can merely curate it, gathering links and images without comment, using the microblog as a repository for either the researcher to consult later, or as a resource for others.

Tumblr (*www.tumblr.com*) is probably one of the more popular examples of a microblogging service (Figure 8.3). It allows users to quickly share a variety of online formats using a variety of methods. Once a user has a Tumblr account, they have access to the Tumblr dashboard, which is not only the area where users post content, but where they can follow other Tumblr users, seeing their updates in a unified interface, rather than having to visit other Tumblr sites or use an RSS reader. From the dashboard, users can post by format, with options for text, photos, quotes, links, audio, and video. There is also a chat option, if a user want to post a chat transcript or overheard dialogue. However, if

Figure 8.3 Tumblr

a user wants to include a variety of formats, the text post option can accommodate formats such as video and photos. The idea behind posts based around the format of the material being shared is to facilitate quick and easy content sharing. A photo post allows the user to either upload or link to an image, give it a caption, and then post. The process for doing something similar in a full-featured blog tool might involve a few more steps.

Tumblr also supports different ways for users to post content. In addition to using the dashboard, users can also use a browser bookmarklet that allows them to post content as they are viewing pages. For instance, if a user sees a quote on a page they want to capture on their Tumblr, they can highlight the quote and click the Tumblr bookmarklet. Tumblr will then post the quotation formatted as a quotation, not only displaying the quote within the user's Tumblr blog, but also including the link for the page from which the quotation originated.

Users can post to Tumblr via email, using a unique email address configured for each Tumblr blog, allowing them to quickly post content to their Tumblr page. While users can post long, thoughtful, well-researched original posts using Tumblr, the service is really intended for quickly sharing material. In fact, one of the built-in features is the ability to reblog something posted by someone else on Tumblr. Logged-in Tumblr users will see a reblog option at the top of every discrete Tumblr post, allowing content to quickly be re-shared throughout the Tumblr ecosystem (and beyond it, as many non Tumblr users read Tumblr-created content).

Tumblr content might have a bit of a reputation for being frivolous, with lots of Tumblrs dedicated to single topics like humorously captioned photographs of the actor Ryan Gosling, pictures of what people eat for lunch, and videos of cute kittens. The reputation of Tumblr might impact how willing certain users are to associate their professional identity with the platform. However, Tumblr does allow users to redirect Tumblr blogs to domains, making it less obvious that someone is posting their content using the Tumblr platform.

Twitter (*www.twitter.com*), the status update service, is also considered to be a microblogging service (Figure 8.4), although Twitter content is even more micro than Tumblr. Twitter posts are limited to 140 characters, making them very short bursts of information. Twitter allows users to post images with their tweets, the Twitter term for posts, but the image does not display with the content and requires users to click into the image separately. Most non-text content is shared via shortened URLs.

This makes sense in the context of Twitter because it's designed to facilitate conversations more than individual postings. Traditional blog posts can stand alone, while tweets often exist in a conversational context, with users

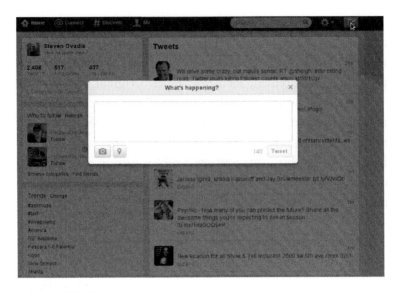

Figure 8.4 Twitter

responding to each other. Even users who do not interact with other Twitter users will need to build up a body of tweets for other users to get a sense of their ideas and work. To frame these services in academic terms, blog posts would be like formal papers or presentations, Tumblr-esque microblog posts would be shorter papers, and tweets would correspond to conference conversations.

Twitter can be divided into two components: tweeting and following. Users posting 140-character status messages are tweeting. The prompt on the Twitter website is "What's happening?" but users are not limited in what they can post, although many choose to answer the question.

Users can also follow other Twitter users, with followed users' tweets showing up in a single interface. One of the many interesting things about Twitter is that it has many interfaces. There is a web interface that is fully functional, but there are also a myriad of Twitter clients for different platforms, both mobile and desktop-based. As a result, it is entirely possible to be a power Twitter user without ever visiting the Twitter website, once a Twitter account has been created.

While there is a tendency to think of tweets as disposable, especially given the default Twitter prompt, the reality is that the quality of tweets depends upon who a user chooses to follow. While the 140-character limitation does not lend itself to sparkling original content, many users regularly post fascinating links to web content, making Twitter an interesting discovery service.

Following is probably the best method of finding relevant content, especially for academics. Twitter has a search feature, but it is not very precise. Many Twitter users make use of hashtags, which are basically subject terms preceded by a pound sign, but hashtags are not required, nor are they used consistently, nor are they a part of a controlled vocabulary. One exception to this rule is that many conferences will choose a Twitter hashtag, allowing an interested user to easily gather conference-related tweets, assuming all conference participants consistently use the hashtag on each tweet.

In terms of finding Twitter users to follow, it is probably best to begin with a general search of Twitter, just to see who is tweeting about a topic of interest. Looking at who the initial Twitter user interacts with will help the user to connect to other users around a topic of interest. It will also allow the user to see who retweets: retweeting is the act of repeating a tweet sent by someone else.

Just as Twitter can be a tool used to follow others, it can also be a tool to allow users to be followed, which might be helpful for a researcher looking to share their work or to develop relationships with similarly-minded researchers. The ability to make these kinds of connections will obviously vary across disciplines, but in general Twitter can represent a way for a researcher to get their name and work out to a larger community.

As a user spends more time on Twitter, they will find themselves following more and more people, and soon keeping up with the various conversations can become challenging. Twitter provides some tools to help users manage the people (and organizations) they are following. One of them is Lists, which allows users to assign other users they are following to lists. Once a user has created lists, they can then view tweets by list. This represents a more methodical way of reviewing tweets. Rather than seeing tweets from everyone the user is following, they can simply view one list of users at a time. For instance, the user might put all of the people they are following into lists based upon the discipline of the person. This would then give the user the ability to review tweets posted from a library science list, for example, separately from a digital humanities one.

As mentioned earlier, there are also third-party tools to help users with their Twitter feeds, with more seemingly arriving daily. Some of these tools are web-based, like HootSuite (*www.hootsuite.com*), while others are client-based, such as TweetDeck (*www.tweetdeck.com*), which was bought by Twitter in 2011. There are also clients for mobile devices and even browser-based plugins that place Twitter information in various parts of the browser. All of these tools help users to make sense of Twitter, which can become quite overwhelming as one follows more and more Twitter accounts.

It should also be mentioned that there are many tools to tie blogs and non-Twitter microblogs to Twitter. For instance, Tumblr can be configured so that posts are also cross-posted to Twitter. For users taking advantage of multiple platforms to share their work, this can be a way to seamlessly share work across services, without having to manually post multiple times.

Users interested in the Twitter concept, but looking to avoid the Twitter platform might be interested in Identi.ca (*www.indenti.ca*), an open-source microblogging service comparable to Twitter, but not nearly as popular. Twitter and Identi.ca operate on separate networks, so Identi.ca users cannot see posts from Twitter users, nor can Twitter users see posts from Indenti.ca users. There are many third-party clients, however, that can integrate the two services.

All of the microblogging sites mentioned in this section are free of charge to use.

Nameplates

Many researchers want a web presence but do not want something that requires ongoing maintenance or updating. Many blogs and microblogs, including Tumblr, allow users to create static pages, where they can share things like publication information and CVs. But an even simpler solution is a concept called nameplate, or landing page, sites, which require very little, if any, technical know-how and allow users to create a site that links to other sites. A user could write a brief biographical statement and then link to their various online identities. For items such as publication lists and CVs, they could link to information on their university site or they could create content using something like Google Drive, or upload information to a service like Dropbox and then link to that through the nameplate site. Many of the citation tools mentioned in Chapter 3 also have a public-facing publication/CV option to allow users to publicly share bibliographic information on articles they have written. For example, Mendeley has a section for publications in the profile area. This allows users to indicate papers and books they have captured within Mendeley that they have also written. CiteULike has a similar feature. Zotero has a CV area that, like Mendeley, allows users to import works they have written into a publicly-viewable CV. These options represent very simple ways to share bibliographic information about works a user has created, without requiring much, if any, technical skill.

For users looking to share basic information beyond what they are able to share on their university site, or perhaps even before they have a presence on a university site, nameplates are a simple way to create a web presence that does not require regular updates. There are many nameplate sites, including about.me (*www.about.me*), which gives users analytics on their nameplate pages (Figure 8.5). There is also flavors (*www.flavors.me*), which has a free tier and a premium tier, with more functionality and options on the premium tier, including site analytics. There are also others, but many nameplate services seem to come and go. Most offer templates and the ability to direct a landing page to a custom web address. Some services are free while others have a charge associated with them. As a genre of web service, these kinds of sites don't always seem to have much

Figure 8.5   about.me

longevity, but there is very little personal data living within them. Instead they are merely linking to existing data. Still, if users are concerned about a nameplate site suddenly going out of business, they might be better off hosting a simple, single web page on their own server, perhaps using one of these nameplate/landing page sites as design inspiration.

Conclusion

The idea of academics being instructed on how to share work and ideas seems, at first glance, unnecessary. Academia revolves around the idea of thoughts being shared, via venues such as publications and presentations. Just about any tenure-track academic in the world is expected to share their work in some form or another. But given the rapid rate at which information is being created, both within and outside the academy, formal outlets are no longer enough for many researchers.

For some, the formal audience is too small. For others, the publication/presentation process is too slow. For these reasons, among others, more academics are using informal channels like the ones described in this chapter to share their work and ideas.

As mentioned previously, some disciplines are more active in these informal channels than others. It is also worth repeating that different institutions take different views of this kind of informal sharing. Many institutions and departments appreciate the attention that this kind of sharing can bring to faculty and to disciplines. For many institutions, this kind of social sharing represents a cost-free way to enhance the prestige and reputation of a department, which can help attract faculty and students. But other institutions and departments see this kind of sharing as, at best, a waste of time, and at worst, an embarrassment. Users interested in using the social sharing tools described in this chapter want to be sure they understand their own academic culture and how this kind of sharing might be received. And, as with all modern social sharing services and tools, users always want to be mindful about what they share and how they express themselves. Faculty and institutions around the world are trying to determine how academic freedom and social media operate in relationship to one another, but there is no definitive answer. Because this technology is so new, everyone within the academy is still trying to figure out what it all might mean. However, the fact remains that more and more academics are choosing to share their work and ideas socially, in addition to via traditional, formal channels.

This chapter has been couched in terms of one-way sharing, where a researcher is using a tool to push their work out to a potentially wider audience than might be had in a presentation, book, or article. But one aspect to this kind of sharing that has not been discussed is the feedback and comments someone might receive when their work is more publicly viewable. Someone might write an article, have it accepted into a peer-reviewed journal, and then have the article published. Others will read the article and have thoughts about the ideas, but the ability of the readers to share their feedback hinges upon their taking the time to either write a letter to the journal or to contact the author directly. Most readers probably will not take the trouble for this kind of feedback. However, the social sharing tools described here are designed to make feedback easier. Many users will be more likely to respond to a blog post or to a tweet, because responding and commenting is so simple in these environments. On the one hand, it is not always advantageous to have a lower barrier to entry in terms of commenting, because the net result might be lower quality comments. But if a user is willing to put up with the potential for uniformed comments and feedback, they might also find useful comments and feedback that will actually enhance their more formal works. While it is not a given that starting a blog will result in feedback, nor is it a given that starting a blog will even result in the blog being read by others, the social spaces described in this chapter make it easier for users to promote their work, getting more readers to see it, and perhaps even to share their expertise in the form of responses and comments. Obviously, feedback is an important part of the formal academic sharing process, but social sharing represents an opportunity to get input beyond what was received from reviewers, with feedback possibly coming from outside a user's discipline, and, in certain cases, perhaps even from outside the academy.

One final note about social sharing: while feedback is one component of the two-way sharing process, another is reading and engaging with the work of others. It is perfectly feasible for someone to share in a vacuum, with a user publishing their work across one or more social sharing platforms, but never reading or responding to the work of others. But many users will discover that as they share their work, they will also come across the work of others. Many times the work will be related, allowing them to exchange ideas across platforms, perhaps even moving the exchange to email, phone, or face-to-face meetings. When a user puts their work out for a large audience to view, it is very difficult for that same user to not take in the work of others. So by sharing work, users also become better positioned to see the work of others, as it has been shared in informal channels. Posting work within informal channels is not just the chance for someone to put their ideas out to the world beyond their discipline, but is also a way for users to take in new ideas that might not yet be appearing or discussed in formal sharing channels. Informal social sharing channels are not only a way for thoughts, ideas, and work to be pushed out; they are also a mechanism by which new thoughts, ideas, and works might be received, extending and enhancing the broader conversations taking place within disciplines.

9

The future of the cloud

Abstract: While the precise future of cloud-based research tools is unknown, there are some possible directions into which the field might evolve. This chapter examines some potential directions for the cloud, including a consolidation of features that might see more services expanding their portfolios of offerings so users become more difficult to attract away. The future of the cloud might also involve a consolidation of customers, with institutions either hosting their own services or engaging the services of cloud providers on behalf of constituents. The future of the cloud might also involve more thin clients, and perhaps might even allow alternative operating systems, such as Linux, to thrive. At the same time, users might rely more on locally-hosted data and/or services, as cellular providers potentially decide to throttle data usage. Finally, given the number of computers and devices many users are managing, eventually a hardware provider might develop a successful single device that serves multiple purposes.

Key words: Linux, operating system, server, tablet, thin client.

The cloud certainly has a role in the contemporary academic world. And right now seems to be a great time for users. There are lots of services, and very few require any kind of financial payment for a usually robust set of tools. Users are free to experiment and see which tools work best for their workflow.

While we're experiencing a veritable user's market at the moment, readers might be curious about what the future of cloud-based services could be. This chapter will use the current state of cloud services to examine some potential futures. Like all forecasting, there is a fair amount of educated guessing involved. Luckily, because cloud services are constantly evolving, there are lots of clues as to the direction in which they might be heading.

Consolidation of features

By now, readers have surely noticed the wide range of companies offering cloud-based services. Some specialize in file management, while others specialize in content capture. Very few services do everything, which forces users to rely on different tools for different tasks. Most users like the freedom to choose the service with features that match up to their needs, but they also appreciate convenience. For many, a service that is not 100 percent perfect is a small price to pay for one less password to remember. Despite the privacy concerns, this is why many users stick with Google. The Google credential provides access to a multitude of services. It also helps that most Google services are of high quality.

Microsoft is trying to position itself in a similar way, linking together tools such as SkyDrive, OneNote, and Word Web App in a way that links content creation to file management, much the way Google Drive now does. Dropbox has not gotten into the content creation/editing game, but the web interface does give users an in-depth preview of files. That might represent the first step toward Dropbox introducing some kind of editing functionality.

Services with only one function might eventually find it hard to attract new users, especially as users become more and more entrenched in their current solutions. The rise of cloud-based services was aided by the fact that users were moving from locally hosted solutions to cloud-based ones. Users were certainly invested in their locally hosted tools, but once they made the decision to move to the cloud, they were not tied to existing cloud tools. To a certain extent, that made movement easier. Many users will become more and more invested in the cloud tools they use and might demand more features out of their existing tools rather than adapting another service to make an existing one more useful. For instance, while the academic market probably is not huge, one has to assume a fair number of academic papers are written using cloud-based word processors. Many users would probably be grateful for some sort of citation management functionality, to make the paper writing process easier. There are obviously many solutions, as Chapter 3 explored, but if a web-based word processor, like Zoho, were to build that kind of functionality into its suite of tools, existing users might be excited, and potential users might be enticed to switch (or at least, perhaps, to try a new service).

Cloud users are getting to the point where they know what they want from services. Existing services might now begin the process of adding those same features in order to hold onto existing users, in the way that Microsoft Office, a bundled collection of tools, has deterred many users from trying new products, since the available and installed Office tools are usually sufficient for most users. Users might also be less inclined to explore new tools as they spend more time with their current ones.

Consolidation of customers

The rise in cloud-based services presents some challenges for institutions. When data is stored on local machines, local IT departments have, to a certain extent, an idea of where data is at any given moment. As more users move to cloud-based services, more of that data moves to the cloud. Local data is often still available where IT believes it to be, but copies of all kinds of information exist on servers IT cannot control or access. IT can certainly block these services from on-campus, but that can be problematic, given how these services are often used for actual work (as opposed to something like Facebook, whose professional utility might be harder to justify).

Faced with the prospect of users with content across a myriad of cloud services, many universities are instead deciding to contract with services themselves, which at least gives IT some control over where user data is going.

Both Google and Microsoft have higher education products that include email, calendars, and a cloud-based office suite. Dropbox has Dropbox for Teams, although its five-user limit is probably much too small for most institutions. SpiderOak has a higher education product designed to support faculty, students, and staff. Organizations adopting these kinds of solutions have more control over how users work with the tools. Users also have more recourse with the hosts than they might with a single free account, because the hosts probably have someone assigned to work with large clients and most of these services would probably like to retain their large clients.

This method of growing a service scales upwards, as even Mendeley – a citation management tool that probably does not have much access to personal data – has an institutional edition. While supporting an entire institution, rather than individuals, is probably challenging for any cloud-based service provider, the financial incentives might make it a more lucrative path. Conversely, institutions probably appreciate knowing where their data is and having a single place to call if there are any issues.

The flip side of this consolidation is in customers choosing to become their own cloud host. Chapter 4 discusses ownCloud, which is software allowing users to create their own cloud on their own server. There is also hardware designed to make web-based file sharing a relatively simple prospect. While these home-based servers are not as robust as the tools discussed in this book, they allow users to share and upload content to a server they control. Users concerned about privacy will find a fair number of workarounds, if they are willing to maintain their own server and if they are comfortable with a product that is not as polished as many of the hosted ones described in this book. Interested users will discover a fair number of web-based calendaring tools that can be installed on a server. Even something like a cloud-based word processor can be replaced if a user has the desire and the expertise. Many users looking for their own cloud-based word processor often experiment with the open source Feng Office. Details can be found at *www.fengoffice. com/web/opensource/*.

The future of the cloud might involve more institutions getting involved in the cloud activities of their constituents, either by hosting services for users or otherwise entering into contracts with cloud providers. At the same time, users might take the same approach on their own, choosing to become their own cloud service, rather than depending upon third parties.

Consolidation of services

Right now is a golden time for cloud-based services. More and more services keep entering the market and while some have a cost element, many of them do not. Users have lots of options and the options don't require a significant financial investment. But businesses require a revenue model to survive. Chapter 6 mentioned a blog post by Pinboard's Maciej Ceglowski that bears quoting here:

> Someone builds a cool, free product, it gets popular, and that popularity attracts a buyer. The new owner shuts the product down and the founders issue a glowing press release about how excited they are about synergies going forward. They are never heard from again.
>
> Whether or not this is done in good faith, in practice this kind of 'exit event' is a pump-and-dump scheme. The very popularity that attracts a buyer also makes the project financially unsustainable. The owners cash out, the acquirer gets some good engineers, and the users get screwed.
>
> To avoid this problem, avoid mom-and-pop projects that don't take your money! You might call this the anti-free-software movement.
>
> If every additional user is putting money in the developers' pockets, then you're less likely to see the site disappear overnight. If every new user is costing the developers money, and the site is really taking off, then get ready to read about those synergies. (Ceglowski, 2011)

The reality of the market is that it cannot sustain an ever increasing number of free cloud services. As the number of services decreases, the existing services might begin to pass more of their expenses onto their users because users will be invested in the particular tools and less in a position to leave a service. Also, as there are fewer options available, users will have fewer choices in terms of other services to use.

A good comparison can be seen in web-based email services. With the rise of the Internet, there seemed to be an infinite number of web-based email providers. However, as providers went out of business, the market consolidated to a few core providers. There remain quite a few free email service providers, but that could be because email is a known technical infrastructure. Many of the newer cloud-based services use newer technologies and frameworks that are not as well-established. As Ceglowski points out, developers need money in order to spend time solving technical problems. Without financial support, developers do not have time to explore new ideas. And without new ideas, it's harder for them to sustain new technologies.

Another future model might involve revenue derived not directly from consumers, but instead indirectly, either in the form of advertising or in the marketing of users' demographic information.

If the past is any kind of predictor, in the future, users will see fewer cloud-service options, but perhaps more stability in the ones that survive. Users might also find themselves having to pay for more services than they are used to at the moment.

Return to local services

Part of what makes the cloud so attractive to users is the access it gives users across devices. Mobile access is by and large made possible by cellular data networks. More and more cellular providers, especially in the United States, are becoming concerned about data usage. As a result, there are fewer unlimited data plans available for users. As users become more dependent upon cloud-based services, and as they use these services on mobile devices, they will find themselves using more data. When users use more data, cellular providers tend to clamp down so users will use less. The easiest way to restrict data usage is to charge users for data used past a certain threshold. In this scenario, mobile access to cloud-hosted data and services could become increasingly expensive.

At the same time, as users become more and more dependent upon cloud-based services, it becomes more likely that they will suffer a catastrophic failure or data loss of some kind. This is not an indictment of cloud-services but more a comment on the nature of electronic data management. As these kinds of data loss situations become more common and more public, users may find themselves maintaining local backups of all of their important work.

In this potential scenario, users might have less incentive to use cloud-based services because of the potential expense or the potential risk of data loss. Either of these two variables, if not both, might be enough to make users return to some kind of locally-saved data implementation. When the cloud loses its convenience, users will probably return to local storage and perhaps to local services, as has been the pattern up to now, with users moving from centralized data and services (accessed via terminals) into decentralized personal computers and now back to centralized data and services.

All this is not to say that the cloud will eventually disappear. Elements will probably always exist because of their utility. So while users might use more and more cloud-based software, the data might be saved on local devices. In this way, users will have access to cloud-based services, but there will be less of a cellular data cost and more data security, because they have control of their own data.

Thin clients

Thin clients are computers with limited functionality that must be connected to a central server in order to function. Readers who remember terminals will understand the concept of thin clients. The model has not had much popularity in personal computing, given how much processing power is available at such a low price. Still, given the variety of cloud-hosted services available, there is a temptation to see whether a fully featured local machine truly is necessary.

Right now, the Google Chromebook might be the most famous commercial, direct-to-customer thin client, although the Chromebook hardware is quite capable of running local programs. Instead, the Chromebook operating system limits users to only cloud-based services. There are no locally installed programs other than the web browser. All other programs are cloud-hosted. Google sells the experience as persistent access to all of the user's work, regardless of the hardware they are using. Even if the user were to lose their Chromebook, all of their work would still be safe in the cloud.

There are other more pure thin client solutions. HP has the ThinPro line of thin clients. Dell also has a thin client line called Dell Wyse. There are also companies, such as Pano Logic, who offer thin client solutions. This type of hardware is not intended for home end-users, but instead needs to be configured and deployed. There could come a time when institutions find the thin client model is more cost effective than the current fully featured deployments. It is also possible that a vendor could come along with a thin client model that appeals to consumers, as Google is attempting to do.

For now, the challenge of thin clients is that users, even users immersed in the cloud, are still used to certain local services or programs. Until users are truly conditioned to using cloud-hosted services with the same convenience with which they use local ones, thin clients will remain a tough sell with a challenging learning curve. However, thin client propagation might be accelerated as cloud-based services get better at mimicking local ones.

The rise of Linux

Related to the potential rise of thin clients is the potential rise of the Linux operating system. Linux is based upon the Unix operating system and has historically been seen as a powerful, common server tool that is also used by some people as a desktop operating system. While there's a wide range of software available for Linux, the desktop software ecosystem has never been able to compete with either Windows or OS X. Because of this lack of commercial software, Linux adaptation has been low, although there are quite a few vocal enthusiasts and public Linux communities. Enough so that despite the low adaptation rate, many of the services discussed within this book have some sort of Linux client. But because so many cloud services are designed to be interacted with via a browser, Linux has become a much more viable choice for users who wish to explore an alternative operating system, for political, economic, or usability reasons.

As mentioned previously, Linux is based upon the Unix operating system. Linux is open source, meaning users can modify it. Linux is also cost-free. In fact, much of the work of Linux is built on the work of unpaid contributors around the world. The fact that it is open source means the code is always publicly available for anyone to use or to work with.

This contrasts with OS X, Windows, and iOS, all of which use a proprietary code base to which only employees of the companies connected to the operating system have access.

Users seem to choose desktop Linux for several reasons. Many users gravitate to Linux because of its open source philosophy. Others choose it because it tends to be more customizable than proprietary operating systems, which need to restrict access to their code for competitive purposes. Some choose Linux because it is cost free, and others because it tends to run better on older hardware, although that depends upon the type of Linux software being used.

A common barrier to entry for Linux for many has always been software. For instance, while there is a version of Microsoft Office for Windows and for OS X, there is none for Linux. And while there are many word processors for Linux, as mentioned in Chapter 5, it can often be challenging to share work between different versions of word processors. But with the rise of services available in the browser, Linux users no longer need to worry about compatibility. A Zoho document will open in any desktop web browser, regardless of the operating system powering the browser. Someone looking to experiment with Linux does not need to worry about finding the right Linux software to work with a file. Instead, they can just use their browser and go ahead with their work.

Just as thin clients are a viable tool because so much work can be done using the browser, Linux also becomes a more viable choice when users do not need to worry about local software.

Devices

Another possible direction for the cloud is a more device-oriented one. Right now cloud services are driven by the need for the same content to be available across multiple devices. Users at home want access to the same material they have at work and, in general, they want some kind of access to most material on their various mobile devices, if only to check a citation or quickly catch up on some reading.

The cloud allows content to be available across multiple devices and locations. But what if there was only one device? What if users didn't need to worry about different laptops and devices? Some users are already at that point, trying to do as much as they can on their iPads. There have been a few attempts to create one master device, although, as of this writing, none has gained huge mainstream acceptance. The Motorola Atrix 4G is a mobile phone that can be docked with monitors or even a laptop, so that it becomes more of a fully featured computing device. The Atrix 4G runs Android as a phone but Linux in computer mode. A similar concept can be seen in the Ubuntu for Android project (*www.ubuntu.com/devices/android*), which allows certain Android phones to run the Ubuntu variant of Linux in computing mode. In this case, a user is using the same device for multiple purposes, potentially making the cloud less important.

In a similar vein, many hardware vendors, such as ASUS, Dell, and Lenovo have netbooks that also convert to tablets. Microsoft, best known for its software, also has a keyboard-enabled tablet called Surface. With all of these convertible devices, as long as a user has their mobile device, they also have their computing device. And eventually their home and work computers could be that single device that also serves as a mobile phone or a tablet. For this scenario to take place, hardware would have to become a lot better, in a similar way to how the iPhone changed how users thought about their phones. Anything less and a user will find themselves with two not-very-good devices instead of one device that does everything.

While the device angle seems a bit far-fetched, many cloud services are thinking about devices in general. In June 2012, Google acquired Quickoffice, a company specializing in productivity applications, such as word processors and spreadsheets, for iOS and Android devices (Wingfield, 2012a). A month or so later, Microsoft announced its next version, which will be optimized for touch screens, as well as cloud services (Wingfield, 2012b). In general, the scuttlebutt around Windows 8, the next version of the Windows operating system, has been that it feels like it's designed for tablets rather than desktop/laptops. Compounding this trend, feedback on OS X Mountain Lion and the Ubuntu Unity interface indicates those operating systems seem oriented for touch screens rather than desktops, and it seems like many operating systems anticipate some kind of consumer migration to tablets and/or mobile phones. It's not out of the realm of possibility to think that these tablet-optimized interfaces are excellent candidates to run on a single device that can serve as a tablet/mobile phone and a more conventional desktop/laptop computer. The main challenge to this sort of device, from the operating system perspective, is that software companies would make less money with one device than they do with multiple ones. However, if a market emerges for that sort of device, you can be sure hardware and software manufacturers will accommodate the need.

Conclusion

The future of the cloud is complex because it involves so many different variables, from devices to cellular providers to users to business strategies. There's no real way to know for sure where the concept is going. However, by considering all of the possibilities, users are better able to protect themselves and to understand the risks and the benefits of the cloud.

It is tempting to imagine the cloud as an endless succession of new services at incredible prices, if not free, but that will probably not always be the case. As services disappear, users will probably have to make do with fewer choices and perhaps more expenses around their cloud-based work. As the cloud becomes a more integral part of work flow, there will be more demanding expectations placed on the services, in terms of features, availability and uptime. As a result of these demands, institutions might take more of a role in selecting and implementing cloud services either on their own servers or on behalf of their campus populations.

Devices will also continue to be an important factor in the adaptation of cloud services. As more users adapt mobile devices for work purposes, users will come to expect more out of the mobile experience. Device power will be one issue, but network connectivity will be another. Can current cellular networks handle all of this data? Will constant mobile connectivity one day be too expensive to maintain? Will users eventually need to choose between huge cellular bills and constant access across devices?

Luckily, the precise answers are surprisingly unimportant in terms of directing the conversation. Users do not need know the exact future of the cloud. Instead, by being aware of the issues relating to the cloud, they are better prepared to anticipate future challenges, as well as to find productivity with future advancements.

Regardless of future directions, success with the cloud depends upon users understanding where their data is and how they can access it. The more locked up data is, the less control users have. The more access users have, including an easy export mechanism, the more options they have, so even as services, devices, and bandwidth thresholds change, users still have their data someplace safe, whether it's a cloud-based solution or a locally-hosted one. When users lose track of their data, they are more vulnerable to being negatively impacted by change. If someone uses a service without knowing how to easily export their data, they are vulnerable should the service go out of business, or should it move to an expensive subscription model, or if cellular access should prove too expensive to be practical. A prepared cloud user needs a relatively easy way to move their data someplace else. Without that ability to easily move data, whatever the data is, the user becomes a prisoner of the service, paying whatever needs to be paid to maintain access, or using whatever device is dictated by the service. For users concerned about the future of the cloud, the best protection against having one's work compromised by the ever-evolving cloud is to understand its strengths and weaknesses. Like any technology, the future of cloud-based services can be managed by sophisticated, knowledgeable users who understand what they are trying to accomplish with the cloud.

References

Allen, D. (2001) *Getting Things Done* (New York: Penguin Books).

Anderson, J. and Rainie, L. (2010) "The Future of Cloud Computing," *Pew Internet*, 11 June. Available from: *http://pewinternet.org/Reports/2010/The-future-of-cloud-computing.aspx* (accessed 2 November 2012).

Bilton, N. (2011) "Taking E-Mail Vacations Can Reduce Stress, Study Says," Bits, *New York Times*, 4 May. Available from: *http://bits.blogs.nytimes.com/2012/05/04/taking-e-mail-vacations-can-reduce-stress-study-says/* (accessed 2 November 2012).

Ceglowski, M. (2011) "Don't be a Free User," Pinboard Blog, Nine Fives Software, 6 December. Available from: *http://blog.pinboard.in/2011/12/don_t_be_a_free_user/* (accessed 2 November 2012).

Chivers, T. (2011) "Mendeley: If you Liked that Research Paper, Try this One," *The Telegraph*, 31 May 2011. Available from: *http://www.telegraph.co.uk/science/science-news/8546833/Mendeley-If-you-liked-that-research-paper-try-this-one.html* (accessed 2 November 2012).

Dawson, C. (2010) "OneNote is Office 2010's Killer App in Education," *ZDNet Education*, 12 May 2010. Available from: *http://www.zdnet.com/blog/education/onenote-is-office-2010s-killer-app-in-education/3924* (accessed 2 November 2012).

Dropbox (n.d.) "How Secure is Dropbox?" Available from: *https://www.dropbox.com/help/27* (accessed 2 November 2012).

Fitzgerald, M. (2004) "Call it the Dead E-mail Office," *Wired*, 7 June. Available from: *http://www.wired.com/culture/lifestyle/news/2004/06/63733* (accessed 2 November 2012).

Garside, J. (2012) "Google's Privacy Policy 'Too Vague,'" *The Guardian*, 8 March. Available from: *http://www.guardian.co.uk/technology/2012/mar/08/google-privacy-policy-too-vague?newsfeed=true* (accessed 2 November 2012).

Gruber, J. (2004) "Markdown," *Daring Fireball*, 17 December. Available from: *http://daringfireball.net/projects/markdown/* (accessed 2 November 2012).

Hardy, Q. (2012) "From a Facebook Founder Comes a Way to Streamline Work Flow," *New York Times*, 20 May. Available from: *http://www.nytimes.com/2012/05/21/technology/from-a-facebook-founder-a-social-network-for-the-office.html* (accessed 2 November 2012).

Heffernan, V. (2008) "An Interface of One's Own," *New York Times*, 6 January. Available from: *http://www.nytimes.com/2008/01/06/magazine/06wwln-medium-t.html* (accessed 2 November 2012).

McCullagh, D. (2011) "Dropbox Confirms Security Glitch—No Password Required," *CNET*, 20 June. Available from: *http://news.cnet.com/8301-31921_3-20072755-281/dropbox-confirms-security-glitch-no-password-required/#!* (accessed 2 November 2012).

Mann, M.D. (2005) "The Inbox Makeover: Secrets of Mac Superheroes," *Macworld*, 26 April. Available from: *http://www.macworld.com/article/1044327/tipsinbox.html* (accessed 2 November 2012).

Mekentosj, B.V. (n.d.) "Papers for iPad," *mekentosj.com*. Available from: *http://www.mekentosj.com/papers/ipad* (accessed 2 November 2012).

Pinboard (n.d.) "Pinboard or Delicious?" *Pinboard*. Available from: *http://pinboard.in/switch/* (accessed 2 November 2012).

Rainie, L. (2012) "Tablet and E-book Reader Ownership Nearly Double Over the Holiday Gift-Giving Period," *Pew Internet*, 23 January. Available from: *http://libraries. pewinternet.org/2012/01/23/tablet-and-e-book-reader-ownership-nearly-double-over-the-holiday-gift-giving-period/* (accessed 2 November 2012).

Ridout, S. (2011) "HOWTO: Edit Citation Styles for Use in Mendeley," *Mendeley Blog*, 3 May. Available from: *http:// blog.mendeley.com/research-tutorials/howto-edit-citation-styles-for-use-in-mendeley/* (accessed 2 November 2012).

Silver, M.A. (2011) "When to Consider Alternatives to Microsoft Office," Gartner, 11 December. (Subscription resource; no accessible URL.)

Smith, A. (2012) "17% of Cell Phone Owners Do Most of Their Online Browsing on Their Phone Rather Than a Computer or Other Device," *Pew Internet*, 26 June. Available from: *http://www.pewinternet.org/ Reports/2012/Cell-Internet-Use-2012/Key-Findings. aspx?view=all* (accessed 2 November 2012).

Sparks, D. (2011a) *iPad at Work*. Hoboken, NJ: Wiley.

Sparks, D. (2011b) *Mac at Work*. Indianapolis, IN: Wiley.

Strohmeyer, R. (2011) "Getting Your Inbox Backlog Back to Zero," *PC World*, 29 November: 32. *Academic Search Complete*. (Subscription resource; no accessible URL.)

Trapani, G. (2006) "Empty Your Inbox with the Trusted Trio," *Lifehacker*, 21 June. Available from: *http:// lifehacker.com/182318/geek-to-live--empty-your-inbox-with-the-trusted-trio* (accessed 8 November 2012).

Wingfield, N. (2012a) "As Google Bets on Mobile Office, Microsoft Waits," Bits, *The New York Times*, 5 June. Available from: *http://bits.blogs.nytimes.com/2012/06/05/as-google-bets-on-mobile-office-microsoft-waits/?nl=todaysheadlines&emc=tha26_20120606* (accessed 2 November 2012).

Wingfield, N. (2012b) "In Nod to New Era, Microsoft Unveils Touch-based Version of Office," *New York Times*, 16 July. Available from: *http://www.nytimes.com/2012/07/17/technology/microsoft-unveils-touch-based-version-of-office.html* (accessed 2 November 2012).

Wortham, J. (2011) "YouTube Founders Revamping a Site for Link Sharing," *New York Times*, 11 September. Available from: *http://www.nytimes.com/2011/09/12/technology/youtube-founders-aim-to-revamp-delicious.html* (accessed 2 November 2012).

Index

about.me, 162
Adium, 136
Amazon.com, 41
AOL Instant Messenger
    (AIM), 132–6
Apache OpenOffice, 42, 45,
    48, 55, 84–5, 91
Apple Pages, 48
Asana, 117

backup, 6, 32, 65, 152, 174
Basecamp, 111–14, 123
bibliographic management,
    33–58
bibliography, 34, 38, 40–1,
    47, 58, 162
BibTeX, 46, 52–3, 55–8
Blogger, 149, 151
Blogs, 148–55, 157–8, 165
bookmarks, 11–32, 40
Box, 70–3, 77, 80

CalDAV, 107
calendar, 91, 104–9, 112–13,
    117, 123, 129, 170
ChatZilla, 139
citation, 4, 11, 33–58, 169
CiteULike, 42, 45–7, 50,
    57–8, 162
Colloquy, 140

comments (online), 153, 164–5
curriculum vitae (CV), 149,
    161–2

data portability, 6, 8, 32, 58,
    63, 181
Delicious, 13–19, 28, 31, 47
Dell Wyse, 175
Diigo, 17–19, 21–2, 27–8, 31
Disqus, 153–4
distraction-free writing, 88, 96
Dropbox, 60–8, 72–5, 80,
    161, 168, 170
Drupal, 151

EBSCOHost, 36, 41, 52–4
email, 60, 64, 80, 91, 105,
    112–13, 117, 122, 127–32,
    144–5, 157, 170, 173
    rules, 130–1
EndNote, 47–9, 57
Evernote, 21–6, 28–9, 31–2,
    125
ExpressionEngine, 151

Facebook, 25, 27, 153–4, 170
    chat, 132, 135–6
    Comments Box, 153
FaceTime, 138
Feng Office, 171

file storage, 59–81, 84, 98–9, 171

Firefox, 20–1, 23–4, 37, 43–5, 48, 58, 88, 116, 139

flavors.me, 162

gedit, 100

Getting Things Done, 108–9, 119, 121

Google, 20, 24–5, 29, 40, 151, 154, 170, 179

Gmail, 109, 115, 128, 130, 134, 138, 144

Google Apps, 87

Google Books, 41

Google Calendar, 105–8, 115

Google Chrome, 20–1, 23, 44, 69, 88–9, 116, 139–40

Google Chromebook, 175

Google Drive, 58, 68–72, 77, 80, 85–92, 94, 96, 102, 138, 161, 168

Google Hangouts, 87, 138–9, 144–5

Google Scholar, 36, 41, 44, 48, 56

Google Talk, 136–8

Google Tasks, 114–16

Google+, 86, 139

hashtag, 159

HootSuite, 160

HTML, 96

iCal (now Calendar), 106–7, 110, 124

iCloud, 20–1, 79–80, 106

Identi.ca, 161

IM+, 136

imo, 136

instant messaging, 86, 132–7, 139, 144–5

Instapaper, 16, 27–8

Internet Explorer, 20–1, 37, 48, 88

Internet Relay Chat, 136–7, 139–44

iTunes, 79

iWork, 79–80

Joomla, 151

JSTOR, 41, 44, 54

LaTeX, 55–6

LibreOffice, 42, 45, 57, 71, 84–5, 89, 92

Markdown, 96

Mathematica for Windows, 48

Mendeley, 39–44, 46, 50, 57–8, 161, 170

Messages (formerly iChat), 138

metadata, 12, 25, 34, 39–40, 43, 45, 50

Mibbit, 139–40

microblogs, 153, 155–61

Microsoft, 168, 170, 179

Microsoft Exchange, 105

Microsoft Office, 29, 71, 77, 79–80, 84–5, 89, 169, 177

Microsoft OneNote, 29–30, 89, 168

Microsoft Outlook, 30, 108–9, 111

Microsoft SharePoint, 30

Microsoft SkyDrive, 29, 76–8, 80, 168

Microsoft Word, 22, 30, 38, 42, 45, 48, 51, 55, 57, 84–5, 89, 91, 93, 99–102

Microsoft Word Web App, 89–92, 100, 168
Outlook.com, 104, 106–7, 134
Surface, 178
mIRC, 140
mobile devices, 4, 8–9, 14, 17, 20, 23, 25, 27–8, 38, 45, 60, 62–3, 73, 101, 107, 114, 143, 159–60, 173–4, 177–9
Android, 10, 14, 19, 21, 25, 30, 57, 67, 70, 76, 89, 91, 96, 101, 106, 111, 137–8, 178–9
BlackBerry, 21, 76, 109, 111
iOS, 10, 14, 19–21, 25, 30, 42, 52, 57, 67, 70, 76, 79–80, 89, 91, 96, 101, 106, 111, 119–22, 137–8, 179
iPad, 21, 49, 79, 120, 137–8, 178
iPhone, 21, 79, 120, 137–8, 178
Kindle, 28
Symbian, 76
Windows Phone, 30, 76, 91, 137
Motorola Atrix 4G, 178
Movable Type, 150–1, 153
Mozilla Lightning, 106
Mozilla Thunderbird, 106
nameplates, 161–3

NeoOffice, 42, 45
Nixnote, 24
Notational Velocity, 100
Notepad++, 99
Novell GroupWise, 105, 108

OmniFocus, 119–22, 125
open source, 78, 100, 152, 161, 176
OpenID, 154
openURL, 37–8, 45
operating system(desktop/laptop), 6, 8–9, 95, 98
Linux, 9, 24, 40, 43, 57, 61, 67, 73, 80, 96, 100, 135, 137, 140, 176–7
OS X, 9, 20–1, 24, 40, 43, 47, 49, 52, 57, 61, 67, 70, 73–4, 76, 79–80, 96, 100, 119–22, 135–8, 140, 179
Windows, 9, 20–1, 24, 40, 43, 47, 49, 52, 57, 61, 67, 70, 73–4, 76, 79, 96, 99–100, 135, 179
organization, 103–25, 137
ownCloud, 78–9, 171

Papers, 49–52, 57
Pano Logic, 175
PBworks, 92–7, 101
PDF, 18, 40–3, 46–8, 50, 58, 63, 88, 93
Pidgin, 135–6
Pinboard, 15–19, 27–8, 31, 172
plain text, 85, 95–6, 99–100
Pocket, 16, 27–8
Postponed reading services, 26–9
privacy, 7–8, 171, 174
ProQuest, 54
proxy, 31, 44–5, 50
publishing, 3
PubMed, 42

Quickoffice, 179

Readability, 16, 27–8
RefShare, 38
RefWorks, 35–9, 42–3, 45–6, 50, 53, 57
Remember the Milk, 109–11, 113–14, 117, 124
reminders, 104, 106, 111, 122
Rich Text Format, 22, 85, 93, 99–100
RIS, 46, 48, 52–3, 58
RoMEO, 154
RSS, 93, 110

Safari, 12, 20–1, 44
ScienceDirect, 36, 41, 54, 56
security, 7
self-archiving, 154
SerialsSolutions, 37
SFX, 37
Simplenote, 95–7, 101
Skype, 132, 137–9
Softaculous Autoinstaller, 149
SpiderOak, 66–8, 73, 75, 80, 170
Springpad, 24–6, 31–2, 125
SugarSync, 75–6, 80

tags, 13, 15, 19, 23, 25, 31, 44, 46, 110, 118, 153
tasks, 25, 104, 109–19, 123, 129
TextEdit, 95
thin client, 175, 177
Things, 119–22, 125
ThinPro, 175
30boxes, 105
Tumblr, 155–8, 160

Trillian for Web, 136
Trello, 116–17
TweetDeck, 160
Twitter, 15–16, 25, 154, 157–61
  Twitter Lists, 160
TypePad, 152–3

Ubuntu for Android, 178
Ubuntu One, 73–5
Ubuntu Unity, 179

version control, 64, 85, 93–4, 102
video chat, 137–9

wiki, 91–5
Windows Notepad, 95
word processor, 2, 26, 48, 55, 57, 72, 83–102, 114, 169, 171
WordPerfect, 91, 99
WordPress, 149–52

XChat, 140
Xirc, 140
Xmarks, 21
XML, 40

Yahoo!, 154
  Yahoo! Email, 134
  Yahoo! Calendar, 106–7
  Yahoo! Messenger, 132, 137
  Yahoo! Notepad, 97–8, 101, 125

Zoho, 72, 91–2, 104, 169, 177
Zotero, 42–6, 50, 57–8, 162

Printed and bound by CPI Group (UK) Ltd, Croydon, CR0 4YY

08/05/2025

01864973-0001